By Jake Porter
June 2015
Council Bluffs IA
Published by YCYOR, LLC

This book is dedicated to the memory of the late Dr. Doug Butzier of Dubuque, Iowa, who was the 2014 Libertarian Party of Iowa Nominee for U.S. Senate. Doug gave his life fighting for liberty on October 13, 2014 while flying back in his Mailbu Piper after a campaign event in West Des Moines, Iowa.

Photo Credit: Dr. Lee Hieb. Taken a week before the tragic accident as Doug flew Dr. Hieb, Don Brantz, and me from across the state to eastern Iowa to campaign with him.

"Never was there a time when I did not exist, nor you, nor all these kings; nor in the future shall any of us cease to be"

Bhagavad Gita

TABLE OF CONTENTS

Before we begin, this is **NOT** another book about libertarian philosophy. There is nothing in this book that will convince you to become a more pure libertarian. If you are looking for a book about libertarian political philosophy, this book is simply not for you. Likewise, this is **NOT** a book about working within one of the two major parties. In fact, I explain the dangers of doing so in Chapter Two. I, for one, do not have the temperament or the patience to deal with Republican and Democrat leadership. Instead, this is a book designed to destroy the stranglehold that the two major political parties have on the American political process and, as shocking as it sounds, one of the two methods I propose doesn't even require libertarians to get elected as partisan libertarians. I know that I just wrote that this book is not about working within the two major parties and now I am saying that winning does not require us to win elections to partisan offices as Libertarian Party candidates. It sounds confusing and contradictory, but I promise that this strategy has been used several times in American political history with great success, and it is actually a large reason we are living in the political nightmare that we are today.

Now that you know whom this book is not for and what the book is not about we should discuss whom this book is for. If you are a Libertarian Party leader, candidate, member, supporter, or volunteer who wants to get our issues implemented then you have come to the right place. This is a book about Libertarian Party political strategy and I am only aware of one other book written about this topic. That was the 1999 book *Stand Up For Liberty* by Dr. George Phillies, a Libertarian activist in Massachusetts who unsuccessfully ran for the party's Presidential nomination in 2008. While this book is similar to *Stand Up For Liberty*, several things have changed in the past fifteen years since George first penned his book.

I designed this book so that any Libertarian Party activist in any state could adopt these ideas in the *Gold State Plan*. You may notice that while the examples I provide in the book are sometimes specific to the state of Iowa, the strategies can easily be adopted by any state. A specific plan for each state would be different based on the state. Some states elect many local offices as non-partisan offices while other states may have partisan elections for local offices. Some states allow voters to register as Libertarians, while some other states do or do not, and some others states do not have voter registration by party at all. Nebraska has only one body (unicameral) in their state legislature, whereas some states like Missouri have elections for County Committeemen that dictate a party structure, and the requirements to become a major party or even get on the ballot are, of course, different in every state. Likewise, in Georgia it is almost impossible to get on the ballot for Congress. In fact, no one from outside a major party has successfully done so since 1943. One could easily write a separate book about different rules in each state. That being said, Libertarian Party activists in every state can use the strategies outlined in this book.

Please note that when I use "libertarian" in lowercase I am talking about the libertarian political philosophy. When I use "Libertarian" in uppercase I am referencing a member of the Libertarian Party. Not all small "l" libertarians are supporters of the big "L" Libertarian Party. Some choose to remain active in one of the two major parties and some have given up on political parties all together. Likewise, as much as it pains me to admit, not all big "L" Libertarians are actually small "l" libertarians. There have been several attempts to turn the party into what I like to call "Republican-Lite" over the years.

These strategies of local organization detailed in this book desperately need to be implemented by the Libertarian

Party in order for us to achieve lasting political success. There is no other option and no other way despite myths some libertarians believe in. The party was founded in 1971 and we have been wandering in the political desert for forty years. Too often we choose to sit in our libertarian debate clubs and discuss political philosophy that we will never implement. This book is designed to get the Libertarian Party out of the political desert, out of our debate clubs, and into our communities and to get our ideas implemented in the political system.

Organizing libertarians is similar to herding cats. It cannot be done by using traditional methods. We cannot have practices that go against our libertarian need to be left alone and to self organize. Additionally, we realize that top-down models are ineffective, especially when dealing with libertarians. We realize that top-down methods are ineffective and inefficient in government and likewise we see that they will not work with our political strategy. This book proposes specific tasks for local organization that allows those local organizations to be established and maintained by local people who will build up the Libertarian political organization county-by-county and state-by-state. This book does not propose a bureaucratic top-down structure that goes against libertarian philosophy and personality traits.

I will be the first to admit that very few of the ideas presented in this book are original. They are ideas from myself and others that I have taken and merged together, and one day I decided that my combination of these ideas had became a somewhat unique and more detailed strategy than anything being used in the Libertarian Party, and that I should write a book about it. The ideas and strategies in this book can be used for years and decades to come. Some things we talk about regarding technology in 2015 will become outdated, but the strategy behind local and community political organization will never become obsolete in our lifetimes. The only things that will become obsolete are the failed ideas and policies of our opponents.

The reason for the name *Gold State Plan* is that the color gold is the Libertarian Party official color, and this plan provides a detailed strategy to one day turn the political maps from blue (Democrats) and red (Republicans) to our Libertarian color of gold, or at the very least, force the blue or red teams to adopt our gold ideas on the issues. To turn our political maps gold, the *Gold State Plan* proposes that there should be a Libertarian county organization in every county in the country. It proposes that we run a lot of candidates and influence public debate. The plan is easy, but it requires a lot of work and dedication. The gold state revolution will not happen overnight. If you are expecting overnight political success, I'm here to tell you that you are going to be disappointed, just as we libertarians have been for the past 40 years.

In fact, it will take at least a decade before we start to see major results or successes, but don't despair. I would rather spend one decade doing real, hard work than spend the rest of my life doing nothing, or worse, spend the rest of my life doing hard work, but using a failed strategy that didn't get the necessary results.

In this book, I describe the strategy in great detail with examples of how it applies to each area of the party. Think of the Libertarian Party like you would a retain supply chain. If one link in the supply chain is broken, it can delay or end the entire process. When every piece of the supply chain is working together, we can run like a supply chain that is able to move products across the world after someone enters their credit card information and presses a submit button on their personal computer.

The *Gold State Plan* requires the state and national parties to help bring local libertarians together. When the local libertarians get together they form the county organizations. The county organizations then hold meetings, are active in the local community, and get members appointed to local boards. They convert members of their community to libertarian thought. They also recruit good libertarians to run for city, county, and state legislative seats. From the local pool of candidates we also find our candidates for statewide and federal offices.

One of the unique features of the *Gold State Plan* is that it doesn't require help from the dying traditional media. Sure, media coverage is nice and helpful, but with the *Gold State Plan* we not only survive, but also thrive with or without traditional media. The media in certain states is very favorable to Libertarians. They mention us and include us in the debates. In other states the media is horrendous. They have been consolidated to the point that a few giant corporations own most of the major media in the state, and if they decide not to mention that you are also running or fail to invite you to the debates it strings a little, but don't worry. If you are active at a local level they cannot easily ignore you, and most small community newspapers are run by real people rather than some impersonal corporation.

Like I mentioned before, the *Gold State Plan* was largely adopted from ideas taken from George Phillies and the Clean State Action Program Committee. I also took ideas from the Partido Movimiento Libertario (Libertarian Movement Party) of Costa Rica. The Costa Rican system was similar to what I am proposing in this book although Costa Rica does not have a winner-take-all system like we have in the United States so it is not an apples-to-apples comparison, but the idea is the same. It is just a little more difficult to implement in the Untied States.

In May of 1994, Otto Guevara founded the Partido Movimiento Libertario (Libertarian Movement Party in English) of Costa Rica as an alternative to the political organizations in the country. In 1998, Guevara was elected to the legislature and spent considerable time improving his skills as a candidate, and by being elected he was able to use the media to influence the debate, which his think tank involvement had been unable to do. Guevara told Reason Magazine in 2003, "I'm convinced that political participation is a much more effective way of promoting freedom than any 10 books you could write." Guevara's party had the same issues that we have with the media, but when they started electing Libertarians the issue was resolved.

Guevara ran for President in 2002 and received fewer than 2% of the vote, but elected 6 of the 57 members of the Costa Rica legislature. He ran for President again in 2006 and the party received fewer than 10%, then in 2010 he ran and received 20% of the vote and almost won the election. Today, the party still holds 4 out of 57 legislative seats.

The *Gold State Plan* attempts to do the same thing that the Partido Movimeiento Libertario did in Costa Rica. We need to run as many professional candidates as we possibly can for the state legislature. In Iowa, for example, 43% of all state legislative races were uncontested in 2014. Think of how many members of the state legislature get arrested or are involved in a major scandal each year. As Barry Goldwater once said of Washington D.C. "If everybody in this town connected with politics had to leave because of chasing women and drinking, you would have no government." If the Libertarian Party runs someone for every race, we are eventually going to win a seat in the state legislature. It has happened 12 times before across the United States and when that happens, the media is forced to pay attention to us. Not to mention, those elected Libertarians can run for higher office with greater name recognition, an improved resume, and a better media profile, which in many states helps us with ballot access in the short-term and eventually makes it easier for us to win election to those higher offices.

CHAPTER 1

HOW
WE WIN

Chapter 1 - How We Win

How often do we hear the same old story from our critics, that the Libertarian Party cannot win so why don't we just join one of the major parties? This sounds good, but it ignores many factors regarding the influence that third parties have had in our past and will have in the future. There are three methods libertarians can utilize to win. The first is to work within one of the major parties, and I explain in the next chapter why I do think believe this is a good idea. The second method is to take enough votes from the major parties so that they steal our ideas. The third method is that we aim to win enough elections to become a major party. We will discuss both the second and third methods in this chapter, and the great thing is that in order to win, we actually try the third method, and if one of the major parties adopt our ideas before we ourselves become a major party, then that is great. If they do not adopt our ideas, we will still eventually win by becoming a major party. It is a win-win situation for the libertarian movement, and doesn't require working within the corrupt two major parties.

How can the Libertarian Party win by receiving enough votes in elections that the major parties adopt some of our most important issues? Has it ever been done before? First, let's look at the Socialist Party. The Socialist Party may not have won many elections, but they were able to get many of their ideas implemented, and their ideas are some of the major reasons we are in the mess we are in today. The 2010 Iowa Libertarian Party nominee for Governor, Dr. Eric Cooper, was a strong supporter of forcing the major parties to adopt our issues. Below, Dr. Cooper eloquently makes his case for the strategy:

> *Third parties can be very successful at getting what they want without actually winning elections. How? The two most successful third parties in American politics (in terms of accomplishing their policy goals) were the Populist party in the 1890s and the Socialist party of the 1910s. The Populists wanted direct election of Senators by the people (instead of the state legislatures) which they got when the 17th Amendment to the Constitution was passed in 1913, and a graduated federal income tax which they got when the 16th Amendment to the Constitution was passed (also in 1913). In the Socialist Party Platform of 1912, they wanted a minimum wage law, laws limiting labor by children, government provided*

unemployment benefits, a government pension program for the elderly, and the establishment of federal departments of Labor and Education all of which they eventually achieved. Neither the Populist Party nor the Socialist Party won many elections at all, and yet they were able to get most of their major issues implemented. How did they do this?

The way they were able to get what they wanted was that they were able to attract a small but consistent group of voters in every election (around 10% is all that is needed for this strategy to work). If a third party can attract 10% of the vote on a regular basis, the major parties will then be tempted to start poaching their issues in order to attract their voters because 10% of the votes is enough to decide most elections between a Republican and a Democrat. A minority of 10% that is strongly committed to their issues can actually be the most powerful group in an election if they are willing to swing their support to any candidate that supports their main issues.

The reason why the time is now ripe for a third party challenge to the major parties is that both major parties have become parties of expanded government.

When I am campaigning, the first thing I ask people is "Do you think the government is too small right now, about the right size, or do you think it is too big?" and at least 70% of the time people tell me that they believe it is too big. Unfortunately, the government has kept growing and growing regardless of which major party is in charge. The last two presidents (one a Republican and the current one a Democrat) have expanded the size of the government more than any other presidents in history. What this means is that if you are one of the 70% of the voters I speak with who want the government to be smaller, you really don't have a major party right now that is willing to fight for that position. In contrast, the reason we are running is because we want the government to get smaller, and a vote for us is a clear vote for small government principles.

Dr. Cooper's plan requires us to run a lot of candidates for high-profile office such as U.S. Senate, Governor, and President to try to take enough votes in elections that the major parties adopt some of our key ideas. I have personally had success with this strategy. I am a two-time Libertarian Party candidate for Iowa Secretary of State and both times

I have ran, I covered the margin of difference between my two major party opponents. I ran in 2010 and then again in 2014. In 2014, the Democrat in my race adopted many of my ideas. Unfortunately, the Republican who won in the large 2014 GOP victory landslide in Iowa did not take any of my ideas during the campaign, but appears to have implemented a couple of minor changes to the Secretary of State's office that I had initially proposed. It is a start. Likewise, during the 2014 campaign I was able to work with the Democrats to fix a voter registration issue that prevented Iowans from being able to register to vote with the Green or Libertarian parties. The reason I was able to do this was because of my success in 2010, and a few Democrats even accused me of "costing them the 2010 election."

The second way the Libertarian Party can win is that we build enough of an organization to overthrow one of the two major parties and become a major party ourself. This has been done before. Did you realize that the Republican Party started out as a third party and replaced the Whig Party? The Whig Party was on the wrong side of history, much like the Republican Party is today. Like the Republican Party of today, the Whigs were branded as an intolerant and bigoted party. This method requires us to run a lot of local candidates, build county parties, win local offices and one day gain enough strength to overthrow the Republican Party as a major political force.

While I agree with Dr. Cooper's strategy of forcing the major parties to adopt our ideas, overthrowing one of the two major parties is the strategy that I personally support and that I believe will be most likely to work as the Republican Party is like an old dinosaur that cannot change. In fact, the dinosaur would make a good new party animal for the Republican Party.

While the Republican Party may be winning elections, their supporters are becoming older and the Republican Party is not exactly able to attract the youth vote going forward. "We're going to send you off to fight in another undeclared war, force you to pay for massive spending programs that will never benefit you, and make your moral decisions for you" is not exactly the message young voters want to hear. The Democrats aren't much better, but their message on the social issues is a lot more libertarian-sounding than the Republicans', although their actions are not libertarian by any stretch of the imagination.

We can accomplish this strategy of becoming a major party by building a strong local organization, and getting Libertarians elected and appointed to local office. Later in this book, we will discuss step-by-step the exact methods of how we will do that, but for now we will briefly review what it looks like.

Becoming a major party depends on your state laws. In Iowa, for example, we must receive 2% in the Governor's race or Presidential race to get major party status, and then receive that 2% every year after that. Most states have different rules. In some states it is very difficult to run as a Libertarian, and it requires a lot of signatures, like the laws our friends in Illinois have. Even worse, in some states the Republican Party is making it very difficult to get on the ballot by challenging our legitimate petition signatures or, even in one case, harassing us by showing up at the homes of people who signed our petitions with guns to intimidate those libertarian petition signers.

Your state is going to have different circumstances under which you can get on the ballot and become a major party, but the general strategy is basically the same in every state, and that is a strategy of building strong local organizations county-by-county, city-by-city, and one day, precinct-by-precinct. With this strategy, we can build up county parties and run a lot of local candidates for city council, county offices, and state legislative races. You may be thinking that most city council races are non-partisan, so how does that help build a Libertarian organization? The answer is that it allows us to implement our libertarian ideas and prevent massive government overreach at the local levels of government, and it puts our members into a position to run for higher office. Think of it as creating a shadow government that could one day be elected to statewide office as partisan Libertarians.

Winning these local offices and implementing our ideas, or at least preventing some very bad ideas, is not only possible, but has been done several times. Nick Taiber has been elected to the Cedar Falls, Iowa city council twice as an At-Large Representative, and Mike Bozarth was a city councilman in St. Joseph, Missouri. Both are potential future leaders that could run and win higher office once the Libertarian Party gets off the ground and starts to win state legislative offices again.

Once we start to win these local offices, we can appoint Libertarians to city boards, and then our county organizations will recruit strong candidates to run for county offices such as county auditor and county treasurer, as well as positions in the state legislature. Having a party with strong local organizations that run a lot of candidates will result in us winning elections to the state legislature and one day impacting major policy decisions.

Now that we have discussed both strategies I am going to surprise you. Both Dr. Cooper's favorite strategy and my favorite strategy could work. However, if I could predict the future I would be retired on a private island somewhere and wouldn't be writing this book. That is why I believe that we should use a combination of both strategies. I propose in this book that we run people for every office and force the major parties to either adopt our ideas or become politically extinct. This means that while we take a local focus, we still run people for higher office. By using both methods we increase our odds of victory. Eventually, the Republicans will decide if they want to adopt a more libertarian message and ideas, or if they want to become the new largest third party in American politics.

We should run candidates for local offices and build up a strong local organization while at the same time trying to impact statewide and federal elections. In addition to impacting the race and getting your opponents to steal your ideas to try to pick up the Libertarian vote, you will also discover that these campaigns for higher office pick up a lot of volunteers and inspire people to run for local office. That is the reason I ran for statewide office twice. It wasn't just because I have an extremely large ego and delusions of grandeur. Rather, running for statewide office allowed me to build the party, recruit more candidates, bring in volunteers, and give our ideas space in newspapers and time on television and radio.

Using both strategies increases the likelihood that we win. It is good financial advice not to put all of your eggs in one basket and the same is true with political strategy. That is why I don't become too angry with the occasional person I run into who wants to work within the major parties to try to turn them libertarian. I think my strategy is a lot more realistic and sane; however, I have to admit that Republican Ron Paul's Presidential campaign probably brought several of you to this point where you are reading my book today. So, while reforming the Republican Party from within may not be possible, it did bring a lot of people to the message of liberty. That being said, reforming the GOP is a Trojan horse that could keep a bigoted, warmongering, fear-based party around when it is past time to stick a fork in it. Notice that if you kill a spider it often has movement after it is dead. This is symbolic of the Republican Party. The movement you see is just muscle spasms of a former national party, and not a sign of a vibrant life ahead of it.

CHAPTER 2

DON'T FOLLOW THE PIED PIPER

Chapter 2 - Don't Follow The Pied Piper

Perhaps at this point you are not convinced of the need for a Libertarian Party and think you can change the Republican Party from within. The idea has some merit, but it is a Republican trap designed to keep us from using strategies of local organization that forces them to adopt our ideas. The Republican leadership wants libertarians to be involved in the Republican Party because it keeps us fighting, using their corrupt primary and caucus rules, and keeps them from being forced to adopt any of our ideas when libertarians take enough of the vote on election day.

The reason the ideas has some credibility is that it has been used before. The Republican Party was largely changed from within during the 1980s when the religious right took the party over from the more moderate and libertarian-leaning supporters of Senator Barry Goldwater, who at least understood the importance of keeping religion out of politics. Some readers will be old enough to remember the fights within the Republican Party over abortion. Today, the issue has been decided within the Republican Party. If you are pro-choice you will likely at some point be called a "baby killer" if you attend a Republican Party event these days. The same holds true for gay marriage. While I believe the Log Cabin Republicans are still around, they are even less welcome in the Republican Party than we libertarians are. Also indicative of current party ideals is the fact that, if you attend many Republican Party events today, you will likely have to say a prayer before events even start.

The simple fact is that the Republican Party needs young libertarians to prop up their dying party. Of course, they will use every dirty trick they can think of to make sure libertarians are removed from party leadership. In 2012, the Ron Paul campaign put libertarians into party leadership positions in Iowa, including state party chairman (although there is an argument to be made about how libertarian the chairman actually is, considering that he said he favored government involvement in marriage). The result of this was that the establishment Republicans, including the Republican Governor, worked hard and in 2014 kicked most libertarians out of the party leadership in Iowa and as soon as they were successful in kicking the libertarians out, they left the convention. The result was that libertarians got to choose the party platform. They were nice enough to let the libertarians pick a platform that will never be followed by Republican Party candidates to make libertarians feel like they were making real political change in the state.

From now on, in every Presidential race, the Republican Party will allow or put up libertarian-leaning candidate to lose in the Republican Party Presidential primary to keep a serious third party challenge from ever occurring. If this sounds like a ridiculous conspiracy theory, look no further than the 2012, 2013, and 2014 elections for evidence that the Republican Party establishment are soiling themselves worrying about the Libertarian Party.

In 2012, the Republican Party challenged the Libertarian Party's Presidential ballot access in several states and, as a sign of things to come in 2016, just this year (2015), the Republican National Committee even filed a challenge against a Libertarian Party lawsuit to allow us to begin collecting signatures earlier in New Hampshire.

Senator Rand Paul has a history of being used to sabotage the Libertarian Party. He even speaks badly about us. "I'm not advocating everyone go out and run around with no clothes on and smoke pot. I'm not a Libertarian. I'm a libertarian Republican. I'm a constitutional conservative," Senator Paul told an Iowa audience in 2013. Of course, I don't run around naked and smoke pot either, and contrary to his stereotypes most of us Libertarians do not do these things, either. In addition to his disparaging comments, he went out of his way to support a Republican candidate for Virginia Governor who supported laws banning oral sex, after Robert Sarvis, the Libertarian candidate, was doing historically well, and followed it up by doing robocalls to libertarians in Florida and visiting North Carolina to hurt Libertarian Sean Haugh these were three of our best races. Not to mention, days after our Iowa Senate candidate died in a plane crash, Senator Paul starred in TV ads supporting the Republican candidate Joni Ernst. I get that he has to work within the Republican Party, but when the only races he focuses on are races in which our candidates are doing very well, you might start to question the motives of the Republican Party.

I'm not here to attack Ron Paul or even Rand Paul. I believe Ron Paul has done great work in moving thousands of young people in a libertarian direction. I commend his son, Rand Paul, for standing up for Americans on the Patriot Act and the illegal NSA wiretapping. I also believe that Senator Paul's support for prison reform is an issue that must be addressed. That being said, he doesn't have a chance in hell at becoming President, and even if he were to become President the only way we can really make changes is by having a strong local organization. Even if Senator

Paul were elected President and governed as a libertarian, very little would change. City Councils would still pass bad laws, states would still regulate people and small businesses to death, and the Congress would still spend like drunken sailors and allow our civil liberties to be trampled on. Only a strong local organization will lead us to lasting political change, and putting our eggs in one basked and making a hail Mary pass with that basket isn't going to do the trick. It is only more nonsense from the libertarians who believe in magic solutions to success.

With all this being said, those libertarians who choose to work within one of the two major parties are not our enemies. It is actually helpful to have several people and organizations such as the Republican Liberty Caucus to fight to elect candidates who are libertarians. It is also not a good idea to have all the libertarian resources in the Libertarian Party basket, so I don't try to recruit or reform them. I just have a difference of an opinion on what is more likely to work.

We shouldn't fight with people who have a different strategy. The Ron Paul movement has been successful at attracting people and the Libertarian Party has not, and it is not because Ron Paul or even Rand Paul have sabotaged us or intentionally harmed us. It is because of our lack of using a strategy of local organization. It also requires us to be able to explain how we can use local organization to win, which will get people excited enough to join us. We in the Libertarian Party can complain all day long, but we have one major problem and someone needs to drag us into the bathroom and put us in front of the mirror so we can see it.

So while the Republican Party has its libertarian supporters tell you that Ron Paul is the only hope and then Rand Paul is the only hope, and in a few years the new token libertarian candidate will be the only hope, I hope you realize that strong local political organizations are the only hope. You are the leader that can make real political change in your local community.

CHAPTER 3

THERE ARE NO MAGIC BULLETS

Chapter 3 - There Are No Magic Bullets.

"Everyone knows what they want the other guy to do for liberty. Do it yourself! If you have a great idea find the resources and the volunteers to make it happen and tell me about it after you have been successful."

2004 Libertarian Party Presidential Nominee Michael Badnarik

There are no magic solutions that will win us elections! In my 11 years of being involved in the party I have heard every magic solution that you can think of and even watched libertarians try several of these magic solutions and fail miserably with each. In fact, I could probably write an entire book about magic solutions for the Libertarian Party that will never work. Most of us probably know that "get rich quick" schemes are too good to be true and do not work. It is no different in politics. Unless we are prepared to have a good plan and roll up our sleeves, we will never be successful.

Libertarians are often lazy. Sorry if I hurt your feelings, but it is the truth. We have looked for magic solutions instead of just doing the real political work, and then blamed everyone else when things didn't change. Now that I have discussed local organization, why supporting the

Republican Party is not a magic solution, and how we win, we have to overcome the fact that we have several "welfare libertarians," as I call them, who are happy to sit back and let others fight for liberty while they tell us how to win elections. While a few libertarians carry all the weight of the party, several libertarians sit back and actively sabotage those libertarians who volunteer their time and money to the cause. These saboteurs are bigger opponents than the Democrats and Republicans because they have done more damage and caused more hard-working activists to burn out than the political system has.

I have ran for statewide office twice as a Libertarian and several people who claim to be libertarians will tell me that we "focus on the wrong issues" or that we could just win if we (insert their magic idea here). The truth is that these libertarians have not run for office, don't show up at events or the state conventions, don't contribute money, won't go door-to-door, refuse to make phone calls, and won't even start a county party, but they still want everyone else to do the hard work for them. A large amount of them cannot even be bothered to register to vote as a Libertarian, but they know how to win elections. You don't even have to ask them to have them tell you what you should do to win elections. The freely give their unsolicited advice.

What is worse is that to try and win the support of these armchair quarterbacks, the hard-working activists will change their message or try their magic idea and it fails every time. The only way to win is to have a winning strategy of local organization and put in the hours and money to make it happen. If someone isn't willing to do the work for the party, they can go elsewhere. We can recruit better and more supportive activists that will help make this happen.

Despite the criticism from the magic solution libertarians, we do not lose elections because we haven't attracted a former Republican Congressman or Governor to run for President, because our issues are too radical, because our social media isn't good enough, because we don't have TV ads, because we lack money, or because of stereotypes against us. We lose elections for one and only one reason, and that is because we don't have strong local organizations. End of discussion.

Why don't we have a strong local organization? Because we have relied on too few people to do too much work on a top-down, no delegation strategy that is not working. We have relied upon bad advice and lazy libertarians to dictate strategy for too long. It is time we try a winning strategy that recruits, delegates, and builds the Libertarian Party instead of one that dreams up bad ideas and waits for other people to implement those bad ideas.

Local organization is simple to do, but it still requires a lot of hard work to make it happen. If you are ready to roll up your sleeves and get to work, I promise that the results will be worth the cost of the hard work required to finally make it happen.

Local organization will work like this. "First they (welfare libertarians) tell you you're wrong, and they can prove it. Then they tell you you're right, but it's not important. Then they tell you it's important, but they've known it for years." as Charles Kettering once said.

CHAPTER 4

BE YOUR OWN LEADER

Chapter 4 - Be Your Own Leader

There is an old Hindu and Buddhist philosophy that I plan to write a future book about that works very well in politics. In fact, political change doesn't work well without applying the philosophy. The idea is simple. You must first change yourself and then, when enough people have changed, the society will change. What we are doing is not really any different. We must first change ourselves, live a libertarian life, and then others will like what they see and change themselves so that they are living the libertarian life of the non-aggression principle.

Libertarianism is not just a philosophy, but instead it is a way of living. Libertarians can be gay, straight, men, women, gun rights activists, motorcycle riders, private pilots, and just about anything else. Likewise, we can think many things are stupid or don't suit our personal or religious beliefs. That is why libertarians are diverse with religious people and atheists both following the libertarian non-aggression principle. I know what is best for my life and as long as you are not harming anyone else, I will not use the heavy hand of government to ever try and force my personal or religious beliefs on you. On the other hand, while I may try to covert you to my way of thought and lifestyle I will never pass legislation to harm you because we disagree. Someone who does not follow this principle of non-aggression is not a libertarian. We cannot change other people if we do not live out our own philosophy.

For years, we have searched for political leaders and political parties to fix our problems instead of working to solve problems on our own. We have waited and expected someone else to do the heavy lifting. It hasn't happened and worldwide this has led to disastrous results. It is obvious that no system of government, political leader, or political party has ever fixed our problems despite thousands of attempts to do so. Six thousand years of modern man has resulted in us moving from killing each other with sticks and stones to being able to push a button and kill thousands of people across the planet in a matter of a few minutes. In fact, when people have tried to put their faith in leaders, we have received charismatic dictators such as Adolf Hitler, Joseph Stalin, Idi Amin, and Pol Pot. In America, we now have reality TV star-type politicians who are more concerned with themselves and the next election, but not about doing what is right. There obviously is a leadership void, but who will solve it?

To see why we have a leadership void we must look at the society. If you want to see the mess this country is in, all you need to do is to turn on the television and watch the news coverage of the upcoming Presidential race. The 2016 race already looks more like a bad reality TV show than a Presidential election. We are not discussing real issues. It is all scripted and is no more real than professional wrestling. We are living in a sociocentric-based society where almost everyone is convinced that their country, political party, church, politicians, and favorite media personalities are always correct and can do no wrong. Anyone that disagrees with our sacred cows is now considered a fool without them even listening to the opposing ideas. There is no way that you could have any political change in a country full of people that will not listen to you. To keep people fighting, we divide ourselves on race, religion, and politics, while the leviathan government continues to grow and violate more of our civil liberties and give all the power and money to big corporations.

The political disaster we are facing is not because of an evil tyrannical government. In reality, it is just a large reflection of the condition of a majority of the individuals living in the country. We have elected politicians who truly do represent a majority of the people. We have the power to vote them out, but we never do. People, like our elected officials, are angry, hateful, and convinced that their lifestyle, political party, and nationality is superior to everyone else. We pass laws without regard to anyone who doesn't hold our personal views. Many people do not help or love their neighbors. Instead of trying to understand and love one another we pass legislation to make others behave like we want them to.

No system of government, no political party, and no political leader have ever granted us true freedom and they never will. The closest thing we have had to freedom was the American Revolution, but even then we found, as Thomas Paine warned, that you cannot free people who refuse to free their minds. Women were still treated like servants, and black people were transported and kept as slaves. The government murdered Mormons and Native Americas. At one point, the government even placed Japanese Americans in internment camps. Despite our political revolution, we never truly gained freedom because we hadn't first freed our minds of sociocentric beliefs.

The leader you have been desperately searching for is not Rand Paul, Ted Cruz, or some other politician.

The leader is you, the individual. The simple truth is that you are your only hope to be free and solve the issues we face. There is no church, no political party, and no politician that is going to do it for you, and until we convince enough people to free their minds of sociocentric beliefs we will never achieve any lasting political change. Even if someone like Senator Paul was somehow to be elected by people who disagree with him on the issues, things wouldn't change that much and we would eventually end right back where we always have in history: big government oppressing people. There are half a million other elected officials in this country who will vote against political change. Just like the American Revolution, if we don't first free our minds then our political freedom will eventually erode.

When you lead your own life by loving your neighbor, helping those in need, and coming up with positive solutions to the issues, people will eventually see your light and do the same in their own lives. When people see you stand up and lead, so will they. When you run for public office it may inspire someone else to do the same. People will start to see the light of us happy and free people who help others and they will join us. Eventually, when enough people decide to become leaders themselves then real and lasting political change will happen. We can solve most of our issues, but average people like you and me who stand up and lead will be the ones do it. It will not be done by changing the system of government, reforming a political party, or a couple of charismatic politicians in whom we have put all of our faith.

Personality cults are dangerous. Hitler, Stalin, and Idi Amin are three great examples of the dangers of following a personality cult. The issue is that there are many libertarians who are not libertarian because they studied the issues and found that libertarianism is the best political philosophy. They are libertarian because someone else who they like told them to be libertarian. Ron Paul is a great example. How many "libertarians" follow his son Rand Paul and change their position to fit his even on issues where he is not libertarian and does not agree with the views they held, before they found out Rand Paul held those views? Please understand, I am not lumping all Rand Paul supporters into this personality cult. Many of his supporters admit that they disagree with him and Ron on some important issues, but believe that they are the best choices. I respect that. On the other hand, I have no respect for someone who changes their position just because a politician they happen to support disagrees with them.

While we do need to avoid personality cults, we still need leadership. We just don't need permanent leaders who are unable to delegate and mentor the next generation of leaders. Some people are natural born leaders, and some are not, but can lead when the need arises, and others are sociopaths who use and abuse volunteers and subordinates, and cause the downfall of their organizations and companies.

We need to find people who are capable of leading, but who do so for the right reasons and who are willing to step down when the time is right. We need candidates to step up when needed and let someone else run when they are ready. Right now, we have several people who have stayed on committees too long or run for office too many times while others are recruited into the organizational structure. After a while, even the best leaders can no longer see or bring us the change we need. They become complacent and the organization starts to die from within.

Later in the book, I discuss in more depth the need to recruit and delegate. We need to look at the two major parties for inspiration. They are literally dying - especially the Republican Party. It is becoming difficult for them to find young leaders to replace their current leaders. Likewise, they are having difficulty with candidate recruitment. One of our greatest strengths is that we have a lot of young people who can move into party leadership roles and many of them will also become candidates in the future.

We must never allow personality cults to cloud our judgment. If someone tells you he or she is the savior of the party, keep them far away from leadership roles and run like hell. We need charismatic leaders that help volunteers, candidates, and activists see their own potential and leaders who are able to bring the next leaders into the party. We do not need sociopaths who want to be a big fish in a small pond.

CHAPTER 5

BUILDING THE POLITICAL MACHINE

Chapter 5 - Building The Political Machine

"All politics is local" Tip O'Neil, Former Speaker of the House

To succeed at either one of the two methods for victory we discussed at the beginning of this book, the Libertarian Party will need to be well-organized, structured, and support and nurture the local groups. That is why we need a *Gold State Plan* for local organization. Like I said before, in other words, the Libertarian Party is like a car. If one piece doesn't work you may not be going anywhere, or in the event you are able to, it may be a very rough and bumpy ride. Alternatively, when everything is working properly, the ride is very smooth and we get to our destination without wandering in the desert for forty years.

In this chapter, we will give a brief overview of the main components of a well-structured and well-run Libertarian Party. I believe, as Tip O'Neil said, that all politics is local; however, local politics still needs a statewide and nationwide support structure. This is why this book discusses the national party. An entire book could be written about the national party. In fact, several books could be written about the national party, but the purpose of this book is local organization and how the national party can foster development of local organizations. Additionally, there are a few other things the party needs that the party itself cannot do on the local, state, and national level, and that includes having fair media coverage and organizations to do political research.

Below, I briefly mention each area of the organization and expand upon each area in later chapters:

National Party:

The national party isn't at this point capable of being a powerful force in politics, and efforts to make it into one overnight are quixotic at best and absolutely fruitless and dangerous to the organization at worst. I served a term as an Alternate to the Libertarian National Committee and I learned that all politics is local. That being said, the national party does have a very important function. The national party must run a Presidential candidate every four years. Not running one would be an unmitigated disaster for our ballot access, membership, media and our reputation. The national party should focus on helping states that are not organized build an organization, helping states with very difficult ballot access laws get on the ballot, and responding to national media stories with a libertarian solution.

With all that being said, we don't want to focus too many resources on the national party as it can only support the local activists. It can never replace them.

State Party:

The state party has a similar, but much more active role than the national party. Its job is to help county organizations form, recruit candidates for statewide and federal office, and help candidates with training, ballot access, and campaign management. Additionally, the state party should take an active role in calling out bad policies proposed by the state legislature and our political opponents.

Once the county organizations have been formed and developed, the state party should take a much less active role in local elections and never act like a dictatorship from the top down, which only stifles growth and innovation of the county organizations.

County Party:

The county party is where the change will take place. The state and national organizations support the county party. The county party does not exist to only support the state and national party in statewide and federal races.

We have had this idea backwards for over four decades and it has cost us greatly. The county party recruits local candidates, runs people for city council, gets involved in civic organizations, and recruits and runs the campaigns of state legislative candidates.

Affiliates:

What are affiliates of the state party? Affiliates of the state party are groups that form to help the state party, but are not county organizations. For example, a group at Iowa State University in Ames, Iowa of College Libertarians would be an affiliate of the Libertarian Party of Iowa, but not necessarily part of the Story county Libertarian Party although we hope members would be active in both. The benefit is that many students on college campuses actually live and vote elsewhere in the state; however, the state party benefits from reaching out to young people at college campuses where we can identify future leaders in the party.

PACs:

Political Action Committees (PACs) will at some point be necessary to help get our candidates elected. The problem with only relying on the state party to do this is that when we rely on one group to do all the work we leave ourselves open to corruption, incompetence, and failure. The reason why this happens is very simple to comprehend. As libertarians, we realize that competition in the marketplace is good and weeds out bad businesses. Why is it that government monopolies such as the United States Postal Service or the Department of Motor Vehicles have the worst customer service and longest wait times? It is not because they intentionally try to do a bad job. It is because they have no competition. Competition forces businesses to innovate and become better. A PAC does the same thing. When the state party is not supporting county organizations or local candidates the PAC can stand in its place and act as a balance to force the state organization to clean their dirty laundry.

PACs have one unique advantage. They don't have to get caught up in bureaucratic procedures that county and state organizations have to. The county and state organizations must remain a fair process for selecting candidates and while that occasionally means that we tolerate bad candidates running for office, it protects the party from a hostile takeover and is a necessary protection. PACs, on the other hand, can focus on recruiting and helping whatever candidates they want even before the party nominates them. This allows us to get an early start on campaigning.

We won't spend too much time on PACs during this book as their role falls outside of the scope of building the Libertarian Party, which is our main focus in this book. PACs cannot be created by the party itself and must remain independent of the party for both legal reasons and to create the level of competition that benefits the party.

Think Tanks:

Organizations such as the Cato Institute, the American Civil Liberties Union (ACLU), and the more local Iowa Public Interest Institute are not a part of the Libertarian Party; however, they do inform us on policy plans and statistics that our candidates may utilize in drafting their campaign speeches, talking points, and issue statements. Likewise, they also alert us to bad legislation that is being proposed in the state legislature and the federal government.

All campaign teams and the state party should work with the libertarian-leaning think tanks to fight bad legislation, promote good legislation, and develop talking points. Additionally, organizations such as the ACLU have fought for Libertarians in the past. For example, it was an Iowa ACLU-sponsored lawsuit that won us our ability to register to vote Libertarian in Iowa in 2007.

Media:

When I talk about media I am not talking about our press releases, or external or internal communications. I am talking about the print, radio, television, and online media. Once again, the party cannot have its own media; however, Libertarian Party members are not prohibited from founding their own media sources. The problem is that while in many states the media is fair to us and mentions we are also running, in some states that is no longer the case. Iowa is a perfect example: in 2010, Iowa Public Television allowed me to debate my opponents. In 2014, I had become such a threat to the establishment that I was not invited despite running a much more active campaign than my opponents had and contributing several thousand dollars of my own money and every weekend for almost a year and a half to the campaign. Additionally, the newspapers that four years ago mentioned I was also running failed to do that in 2014. Dr. Doug Butzier, our candidate for U.S. Senate, was told he was not newsworthy by KCCI, the local CBS affiliate out of Des Moines, but they were one of the first to report his death in a plane crash three weeks before the election, which became a national news story. It is amazing that in order to even be listed as also running in Iowa you have to die in a tragic plane crash.

Now, most of us are not rich enough to buy or start our own TV or radio station; however, print media is dying and starting an online newspaper isn't that difficult. It is outside of the scope of this book to discuss how we form our own media; however, getting involved in the media industry and starting your own publication can earn you good money and is something Libertarians should consider. The key is to hire local people to report on news and, at the very least, make sure your publication mentions that the Libertarians are also on the ballot.

CHAPTER 6

GROWING MEMBERSHIP AND BASE OF VOLUNTEERS

Chapter 6 - Growing Membership and Base of Volunteers

There was an old joke that when the Libertarian Party first started to become active in the 1970s, the local police in Los Angeles decided they needed to find out what this new party was all about. The lieutenant sent out an officer to infiltrate the new local Libertarian Party. When the officer reports back, the lieutenant asks if he was successful. "I don't know. They elected me chair," was the response from the officer. Actually, after my time in the party, I am not certain if it is really a joke or not. I have watched new volunteers elected to party positions and become federal candidates over the course of a single meeting. In an organization that is just starting out, sometimes it is necessary, but that needs to change going forward.

In every state, we still have a top-down structure with too few volunteers trying to run operations for the entire state. The larger the state geographically, the more difficult this becomes and the more resources the few volunteers we have must spend. Eventually, after we get the county organizations established, we will be able to cut back on the resources needed at the state level to recruit candidates, and their resources can go towards lobbying, managing lists, and data for the county organizations.

Membership is discussed in more detail a little later in the book during the chapters that look specifically at the local, state, and national levels. I discuss how the change in the membership system collapsed some state parties, and the need for each state party to define membership based on their circumstances and, often, on state law. For example, in Iowa, when we become a major party, state law will no longer allow us to have memberships to vote on internal politics, as the Iowa Code states that registered voters are members of a major party. With that said, we can still offer club memberships with certain benefits not available to people who are simply registered as voters with the party. There are issues with hostile takeovers one has to watch out for. All of that is addressed a little later on, but in this chapter we look at increasing membership and volunteer levels.

Why do people not become members? We must first look at where our support comes from. From my analysis we do best among voters between the ages of 18-35. This is our support base from which we should work to get members. I also should note that in high school mock elections, I received three times the votes that I did in the general election. In four years, all those kids will be old enough to actually vote Libertarian, which means if I were to run again in 2018, I should receive even more votes than I did before. Compare this with the Republican Party. The Republican Party is literally dying off, which I explain more in the next chapter about growing the voter base.

Now that we know where our support base is from, we must ask why our membership levels, particularly at the national level remain stagnant? There are a few possible reasons. For one, direct mail is very ineffective at reaching young people. Another reason is that young tend to have less money to spend on political party memberships when they are just trying to be able to afford to put food on the table. They often haven't had the opportunity to build wealth when they are saddled with student loan debt. Of course, the standard $25 for membership that many state parties charge is not that much money. Another reason is that while many of these young people vote Libertarian, but they believe in working within the Republican Party.

I have said before that I don't think it is, for the most part, beneficial to try to work within the Republican Party. I can respect that others disagree. I can also admit that I was wrong in the past. Ron Paul's 2008 Presidential campaign brought the libertarian philosophy to a lot of people and if you are reading this, there is a good chance that you are one of those people. At the time, I didn't think him running for President would change one thing. I was wrong.

Today, I believe, as I said in a previous chapter, that the Republican Party is using us to do their dirty work and keep young people involved in a system that is never going to let us win. That being said, I cannot blame young people for not joining the Libertarian Party. We should look at the facts: we haven't elected anyone to the state legislature in over a decade. We haven't won in the marketplace of ideas, as George Phillies would call it. We have done an abysmal job of explaining the strategy of how we win. When most young people look at the Libertarian Party, they don't think we can win and when we spend all of our time complaining about how corrupt the system is, we paint that stereotype of us being perpetual and perennial losers. The fact is that we can win, but we first have to convince people that our strategy doesn't even require us to win elections, just like the socialists did in the 1900's. Sure, getting 3% of the vote and winning a bunch of city council races doesn't sound sexy, but it works and long-term it will have more impact that election two or three Congressional Republicans who lean libertarian.

The way we get people to become members and join us as volunteers is to build up the local organizations. It is just like the saying on the Field of Dreams: "If you build it, they will come." When you have a lot of candidates and county organizations that meet, a lot of people will slowly trickle through the doors. Over a short period of a few years, many of these people will become members.

I should also note that a volunteer is much better to have than a dues-paying member that only gives $25 a year. We cannot beat the major parties on money. Trying to do so is a recipe for failure. They have more money and special interests than we can ever possibly have. You cannot easily bribe someone who wants to get government out of giving tax breaks to big corporations. Also, local organization doesn't require a lot of money to run the operations. Local organization doesn't need to waste money on traditional media advertising done top-down that has no impact. Instead, local organization relies on local people to get out in their communities and reach the voters one by one. It plays to our strengths and ignores our weaknesses.

So how do we get these volunteers that are active in their local communities?

Why do people volunteer? It depends on the person and largely on their personality type. Some people, like myself, do so out of a civic responsibility. I do it for the same reason that I don't litter and choose to donate blood. Others will do so if they can do fun activities and use it as a social time to make friends. When I first joined the party, that wasn't really possible. There were very few of us. Today, there is a huge social aspect of being involved in the party, as our numbers of registered voters and volunteers have exploded in the past few years. Some will do so to intern and build skills for future jobs. Some will start as volunteers and learn the process and one day run for office. It is important for the local chair to find out what motivates someone and use that as a selling point to get the individual active in the party.

If someone likes to make phone calls, let them make phone calls. If they want to stuff envelopes, let them stuff envelopes. If someone wants to go door-to-door, let him or her go door-to-door. There are myriad tasks, from gathering petition signatures for ballot access, editing press releases, maintaining lists, hosting events, and just about everything else you can think of that always need volunteers. If someone hates doing something, don't burn them out and scare them away by giving them that task.

It is important to realize that only about 10% of people who volunteer will actually show up and do work. The average life of a volunteer is two years. Well, not their actual life fortunately; volunteering rarely kills people, but their time active within the party is, based on my years of experience, just two years. The reason is often that people, especially young people, get busy with their new careers and families and have to briefly step away. Sometimes they come back. Others get burned out from doing all the work and many of the lazy libertarians do nothing but criticize them while throwing more work at them. Others have unrealistic expectations and don't realize how we win through local organization without needing to win major elections. They become disappointed after several losses and give up.

Once you build the local organizations and keep people active and motivated, the membership and volunteer issues largely take care of themselves. People want to be part of a winning team. Until we explain how we can win and brand ourselves as winners and quit whining about how difficult we have it, no one will join us. People join the

Democrats and Republicans because they win. They pick what they think is the lesser of two evils and join a winning team. If they only understood how much power a protest vote for the Libertarian Party holds, they would never waste their vote by voting for the Democrats and Republicans again.

CHAPTER 7

ESTABLISHING A STRONG VOTER BASE

Chapter 7 - Establishing A Strong Voter Base

How do the Democrats and Republicans manage to do well in elections that they do not even campaign in? How do they find candidates to run in areas in which they are not really strong or organized? The answer is that they have a strong base of supporters that can be counted on to show up and vote on Election Day, and from that base of supporters they find candidates who are placeholder candidates to run for office. Following the *Gold State Plan* requires us to start building our own base of Libertarian Party voters.

One of the major benefits the Democrats currently have is that they will likely win the Presidential elections for many years to come even though they may lose the House and Senate. The reason is that their former Democratic National Committee Chairman Howard Dean decided they would take a 50 state strategy and organize in areas of the country they previously had no chance in winning. Critics called Dean's strategy foolish and didn't think it would work. Dean could see changing demographics and realized that in a few years, some states would become swing states that had not traditionally been swing states. The results have been nothing short of impressive and, for us, inspirational.

Just look at an electoral map to see how large of a margin President Obama won by in both 2008 and 2012. We are not going to have any areas that we win major elections for a while. That is why we must start organizations in areas where we are not currently strong.

A great example of this has happened in Iowa. Ed Wright, a long-time activist has been active in his county for over a decade spreading libertarian thought. When Ed ran for Congress in his first race, he received 8.2% in his county in a four-way race with another libertarian on the ballot running as an Independent! These results were amazing. Even better, he helped other candidates on the ballot. For example, I did better in Guthrie County than I did in any of the other 98 counties in the state. While Guthrie County doesn't have a lot of active libertarians, it does appear to have a strong Libertarian-voting block. From that voting block, we can one day recruit other candidates, and it helps our Congressional and statewide vote totals even if we never win the majority of votes in Guthrie County.

Your state may or may not allow voters to register as Libertarians. If your state does, your job is a lot easier. The registered voters in each county can help form local groups, you can merge lists to determine the best locations to ask your registered Libertarian voters to put up yard signs, and you can determine if your outreach is actually growing your party membership. The lists also make it easier to help with absentee voting if your state allows or encourages it, and helps the "get out the vote" efforts by getting your voting block to the polls.

We grow the voting block anytime we run good candidates who can articulate the libertarian message in a way that other people can get behind. We grow this voting block by being mentioned favorably in the local newspaper articles, going door-to-door, showing up at the local parades, getting on talk radio, and the local TV news. Additionally, the voting block expands through efforts by outside groups and people that convert others to libertarian philosophy such as Reason magazine, the Cato Institute, and John Stossel.

Growing our voting base takes a lot of time and effort. It is why a candidate for office should speak to high school students who are not even able to vote. In just a few years, they will be old enough to vote and there is a very good chance we can recruit them to volunteer and become members. There is an even better chance that we can recruit them to join our voting base where they may or may not give us money or volunteer, but we can count on them to show up and vote for the rest of their lives.

There is a huge benefit to getting people to become a party voter at an early age. Most people change political parties only once or twice in their lifetime, if that. People stay with their political parties often longer than they stay with their spouses. This is the reason why the Libertarian Party has much more difficulty converting older people than younger people. People do not like change. It scares them. It is easier to get someone to register to vote or to become a base Libertarian voter in their first election than after they have became accustomed to voting a certain way for the past forty or fifty years.

By growing the voting base for the party in a county-by-county effort, we will get to the point of having a strong but decentralized party that has major influence in not only local and county offices, but Congressional, statewide and even someday perhaps national elections.

CHAPTER 8

IMPORTANCE OF RECRUITING CANDIDATES

Chapter 8 - Importance of Recruiting Candidates

There is a debate within the Libertarian Party about how many candidates we should run. If we run a lot of candidates we stand a higher chance of some of them performing badly, embarrassing the party and setting us back. On the other hand, we still run that risk when not running as many candidates, and a few bad apples make a much larger impact on a small group of candidates. Additionally, we honestly do not have the necessary resources to help the candidates we do have. Won't running more candidates hurt the candidates we already have?

We do not run into these problems because we have too many candidates or too few resources. We run into this problem because we are trying to make it happen by using a top-down bureaucratic structure that is unnecessary and will only burn out the candidates and party leaders that we have. The end goal, of course, is to run a serious and credible Libertarian for every office in the country, but even the Democrats and Republicans cannot achieve this goal. In fact, in some states most offices for state legislature go unchallenged, so that is probably not a realistic goal to have.

The solution is that we build strong local organizations that independently recruit and support as many qualified and good local candidates as possible. The more candidates we run, the better chances we have at winning elections and influencing public policy. In addition to running as many good candidates as possible, we should also try to get our members and registered voters appointed to local boards that decide public policy. Most mid-size-to-large cities have several city boards that decide important issues such as zoning, housing, and regulation of rental properties.

The great news about running candidates for local office is that in many places the offices are non-partisan, meaning that you don't lose elections to the ignorance of voters just voting for one of the two major parties. Another major benefit is that voter turnout is usually very low for city council races in most parts of the country, which means that if you have built the dedicated support and have a voter base who gets out to vote in city council races, you can easily elect libertarians to public office.

By running a lot of candidates we put ourselves in the position to win elections that we currently see as unwindable. According to what sources have told me, we have elected 12 Libertarians to the state legislature in the states of New Hampshire, Vermont, and Alaska since the party was first formed, and had a 13th one change his voter registration from Republican to Libertarian after a drunk driving scandal. These elections are winnable if we run in enough races. How many of the major party candidates are arrested for drunk driving, domestic abuse, or fill out paperwork improperly each year and only win because they were running unopposed? I don't have the number, but Libertarian Jeremy Walters was an example of how well Libertarians can do when our major party candidates make a mistake. Walters lost the 2012 race for South Carolina state legislature by 3 percent after his opponent didn't properly fill out their paperwork.

Of course, running a lot of candidates means that occasionally we will have our own scandals, and because of that, one question that frequently gets asked is how we vet our candidates. I can give you several examples of bad Libertarian candidates that have run. Some were not really libertarians. Others were just embarrassing, like the one candidate that went a little overboard with some colloidal silver and turned himself blue. It is sad, but interesting to note that these candidates often do very well in elections.

That being said, we want to do as much as we can to keep the tinfoil hat enthusiasts from running for office.

The best way is to discourage them from running and, if they do decide to run, we need to have a base large enough to primary them. We don't want to get to the point where we get establishment leadership from the state or national party dictating our candidates like what happens in the major parties, and that means that it is up to us to make sure that we vet our candidates in the nomination or primary system that we have in your state.

Vetting should not be used as a litmus test for candidates, but should be used to give information to party members and voters who decide if we should place them on the ballot or not. Common things to look for include whether the potential candidate has any prior arrests for harming another. Libertarians should remember that a criminal conviction for a victimless crime such as marijuana possession should be considered differently than a conviction for child molestation, armed robbery, or murder when vetting. Have they run before? What is their stance on the issues? Do they support libertarian stances on the issues? Do they look and act the part? Hopefully, we can determine that they are respectful and don't come across as hateful or angry to the average voter.

Even with proper vetting some scandals develop during the campaign. I know from personal experience where I was Chair of a campaign in which the candidate was charged with sexual assault. Having the charge thrown out after the election and after the news story broke was too late to help us. Also, in some states, if they collect the signatures they are on the ballot and there isn't a whole lot we can do to stop them until we get major party status.

The key is to run as many good candidates as possible so that when you do have a bad one run, all the good candidates we run overshadow them. By running as many good candidates as possible, we will start to win elections. Several libertarians have proven they can get elected and then re-elected to non-partisan offices and make a real impact. Getting elected also makes it more likely that they can one day get elected to a partisan office with a big L next to their name on the ballot.

CHAPTER 9

INFORMATION TECHNOLOGY -OUR SECRET WEAPON

Chapter 9 - Information Technology-Our Secret Weapon

S ince we have a large number of young supporters in the Libertarian Party, we can utilize them to build a strong technological infrastructure for the party that is not only on par with the Democrats and Republicans, but actually beats them. The new wave in technology allows for information to be spread without using many financial or volunteer resources. This keeps volunteer time and money free for other political activities.

The Democrats' and Republicans' ideas are stuck in the 90s. The 1590s. The technology the Republicans use is often stuck back in the 1990s. The Democrats are a little better, but they still have issues with using outdated technology. The fact is, they are top-down structures that cannot easily adapt to change. With a local organization, we can easily adapt to change, especially considering how many young volunteers we have that understand the technology we are using.

How can we use technology? The key thing to remember is to keep everything simple. We need to have databases, websites, online discussion forums for executive committee members, conference calls, social media response teams, and e-mail lists. We just need to integrate all these components into something that works together. I will show you how, but I am not going to go into great detail, at least not in this book, as the technology will change and while the summary of how to do it will stay the same, the programs and content management systems used will likely change in a few years.

The first thing we start with is a website. I recommend having one website in the state that all county parties and affiliates can use. The website connects all functions together. I recommend building two websites, as the website has both an internal and external function or, even better, integrating the internal website into the external website with the option for protected login information.

The internal function allows us to store all meeting minutes, discussions for our executive committees, contact information for volunteers, voter files, media lists, task lists, and the ability to send mass e-mails to voters and media contacts, to name a few.

The external website, the one that voters actually see, has a few main objectives, and most websites get it wrong. As I write this, there is a large exodus away from people visiting websites and instead visiting Facebook pages. Your state party still needs a website. The key is to link the website back to the Facebook and Twitter pages to integrate them. The goal is to design the social media pages so that people can easily click on links to get back to your website where they can sign-up for your e-mail lists, make donations, and volunteer. The website also has a critical media function. When stories are developing, reporters will often search for websites to see if they can find contact information and press releases. They also use photos on the website for breaking news stories. For example, when our Senate candidate passed away right before the election, the media used a photo from our state party website. The website must look just as good as the Democrats' and Republicans' sites in your state and include the necessary information listed below:

Candidates - Links to candidates' websites

Contact Us - A page to contact the state party

County Party and Affiliate Pages - Separate pages for each county party and affiliate to post events and news.

Donations/Memberships - Your website should have an address to which people can make out checks, and it should be able to accept online donations

E-mail Sign-Up - A form to sign-up to your e-mail list

Media - Links to press releases, and someone for media contacts

Volunteer Sign-Up - An online forum for people to sign up to volunteer

The old and outdated way of doing things was to have a webmaster keep the website updated. With improvements in technology this is no longer necessary and it would be an expensive nightmare to set-up all the necessary county party and affiliate pages that way. This is why websites should use a content management system such as Drupal or Wordpress (both are free) to build the website. Drupal and Wordpress allow you to have multiple logins for people to make changes to the websites based on permissions. With a little customization, you can grant specific access to edit pages to people you choose based on their roles. This means that you can keep the website secure while not requiring one person to make all the updates.

Imagine the disaster of trying to maintain several county party websites. What happens if there is a disagreement and the county party splits into two? How about the added expense it costs? In states with several counties such as Iowa, it would be difficult for the state party to help maintain and it would be very expensive for the local groups, with each paying about $100 a year for the domain and hosting. The easiest way to fix this problem is to create a separate page for each county party on the state party website. It saves time, money, resources, and makes it easier if a county party disaffiliates, as the state party can take back over the page.

Each county or affiliate should be able to post a blog, news, events, and link to their Facebook or social media pages. They should also be able to use the state party's internal website to store all of their meeting minutes and county party chair or affiliate chair contact information. Additionally, each county party should receive the volunteer and e-mail list information of anyone signing up for the volunteer or e-mail list in their county.

Candidates should still have their own websites. It brands them individually and allows them greater freedom to run and manage their own campaigns. With that being said, the state party website should still list the candidates on their website with a link to their social media pages and website, and include a professional photo and short biography for each candidate endorsed by the party.

The social media pages for each county party should, whenever possible, have a couple of administrators and be set up by the state party. The reason is not to make it a top-down organization, but to control fights over ownership of the pages and to replace the administrators if they lose access to their social media accounts that maintain the page. The local groups would still be responsible for positing to and administering their group. Realistically, this will not always be the case. As we do not own Facebook, we cannot control if someone else starts a county party Facebook page on their own.

We have to be careful about who we let post on the pages. A racist, sexist, or offensive comment could be used to discredit us. Likewise, we want to have content that reflects the fact that we are both socially tolerant and fiscally conservative. We don't want all content to be on social issues or, on the other hand, all content to focus on economic issues.

The purpose of the e-mail lists and social media pages are to get your supporters to take action quickly. For example, imagine an important bill that will impact the ability of Libertarian candidates to get on the ballot has just moved out of a committee and is about to be voted on by your state legislature. A quick response on social media and to your e-mail list may make the difference between the bill passing or not by having enough people get involved and lobbying for or against the bill. The other purpose of e-mail lists and social media pages is to invite supporters to attend their local events. Just remember, don't spam the lists. If you don't have anything important to say, don't say it.

Databases:

Now, let's move onto talk about databases. We will look at what types of data you need to collect, store, and distribute, and how it helps the party and our candidates.

There are several types of data the state party should collect and distribute out to candidates, volunteers, and county parties. These include the following:

Donor List

Media List

Membership List

Registered Voter List

Volunteer Lists

All these lists are important. Below we will look at each one individually.

Donor List and Membership Lists: The donor list is important for fundraising purposes. You want the donor list to be accurate and include information on what causes the donor to give, if that is possible. Is there an issue that causes them to donate? Do they donate only in election years? The membership list is very similar. You want information such as mailing address, e-mail address, and phone numbers to be up to date. I have stories about dead people remaining on Libertarian Party lists for over half a decade. Unless you live in Illinois where the dead can still vote, this is unacceptable.

Media List: Media lists should be purchased. Some companies sell statewide media lists for under $100 depending on the size of your state. While the technology exists to easily merge them into an e-mail list to send out blast e-mails to every media contact in the state **DO NOT** do this. Only send the media news releases that are relevant to them. In the appendix, I have attached two sample press releases that received a lot of attention from the media. I discuss handling the media in much greater detail in Chapter 11.

Registered Voter List: If you have a plan for it, the state party should collect an entire voter registration list, in an Excel spreadsheet format, from the Secretary of State's office for all active registered voters for the last four years. The lists should then (of course, make certain you are following your state's rules in doing this) be broken down and distributed to local candidates and every county organization. It doesn't stop there. The county organizations should use this list to help place yard signs. Additionally, the local candidates and county parties should look into purchasing software that allows them to upload the lists, find their base of potential supporters, and have their volunteers to go door-to-door canvasing. Some software is innovative enough that it gives volunteers a map, and when a door is knocked on, volunteers can mark it off with an application on their smartphone. Likewise, some of the software can be used to allow volunteers to call from their home computers with a script.

Volunteer List: Like the registered voter list, the volunteer list should be shared with county organizations and local candidates who live in the area where the volunteers live. The volunteer list needs to be easy to edit and maintain. I recommend using Google Drive for the volunteer list. It is easy to embed on most websites and allows you to easily collect information from those signing up. The volunteer list should include the volunteer's name, address, phone number, e-mail address, and information about what they would like to do. Contact the volunteers back! It should also have a spot or perhaps even a separate form for those interested in running for office. Remember, we are not a secret society. We want people to join us! We should make it easy for them to do so.

Other Lists:

Media should be allowed to sign up for press release distribution lists, and volunteers should be able to sign up for a general e-mail list that lets them know about important events in their areas and action alerts. It is a good idea to have these lists on the front page of the website and linked on the social media pages.

Before I finish this chapter I must mention a few brief notes on security. A lot of state parties and candidates have had issues in the past by not owning their own domain names for their campaign websites or by having all the website permissions granted to one person. In fact, the Iowa Republican Party lost access to their website, Facebook, and Twitter pages for over a month in 2014 when a staffer allegedly didn't hand over the login information after being forced out because of inner-party politics. By giving multiple people access to the website and making regular backups you can prevent many of these issues.

I will also remind you to be very careful about buying expensive software, especially from people who are members of the party or executive committee members. A lot of times, people can use their party influence to get the party to give them a contract that doesn't meet its objectives and ultimately costs the party a lot of money.

CHAPTER 10

INFLUENCING PUBLIC POLICY AND USING THE MEDIA

Chapter 10 - Influencing Public Policy and Using the Media

W hy do we run for offices that we cannot win? Why not only run for local office? The answer is simple: we run for these unwinnable offices in an effort to influence public policy and, in some states, to help with ballot access for down ticket candidates. One method is, as I mentioned before, to get our opponents to steal our ideas. I have already explained that in great detail. In this chapter I want to discuss how we can use our campaigns to educate voters on the issues and how we can use media and advertising to change public policy.

In 2014, when I ran for Iowa Secretary of State for the second time, I was able to influence two major issues. One of these issues was directly related to the office and the other was not. I will explain both and how I was successful.

The first issue I worked on was fixing a voter registration problem that prevented Iowans from registering to vote as Greens or Libertarians at the Department of Motor Vehicles. Thousands of Iowans had been impacted and the Secretary of State's office told me and others that they couldn't find an issue, and it was isolated to a few individual cases. I had moved back from Nebraska to Iowa and it happened to me. I had reports of it happening to several people. I started making calls and built a database of over 30 people that had their voter registration changed from Libertarian to no-party. I asked the Secretary of State's office to fix it. No response. I sent out a press release and then I realized that the Secretary of State was a Republican. I contacted the leadership of the Iowa Senate Democrats who oversaw the Secretary of State's office. As I suspected, it was an error in their programming code. Likely an accident. Within a week the Secretary of State's office called me, fixed the issue, and sent out a postcard to every voter they could find that might have been impacted. This was a major victory for the Libertarian Party of Iowa and at that point I had already won, even if I were to drop out at that point.

The second issue I had a major impact on had nothing to do with the Secretary of State's office, but was something that I felt like I had to do something about. Benton Mackenzie, a 48-year-old man, was facing a mandatory minimum prison sentence for using medical marijuana to treat his angiosarcoma, a rare form of cancer. Additionally, the state of Iowa was attempting to prosecute his family for allegedly concealing his marijuana use. I debated not doing anything because it didn't relate to the Secretary of State's office, but I had a small microphone and I couldn't watch this happen without saying something. I put out a series of posts on Twitter noting how the Iowa Governor had pardoned turkeys and pigs, but wouldn't pardon a dying cancer patient. The story was picked up by a local television news station in Des Moines and the next thing I know, a supporter was getting me on talk radio to discuss it. I even worked with our candidate for Governor, who then took the case to a larger audience. The Mackenzie family avoided jail, but sadly Benton was denied his medication and died in January of the following year. Also, his friend who allegedly helped him grow the marijuana plants was prosecuted for his so-called crimes. While I wish we could have done more, I am proud of what we accomplished and while the state legislature didn't pass a medical marijuana bill in the state house, the state senate did and approval ratings for medical marijuana skyrocketed after the story.

Influencing public policy is a major victory for us. While you cannot make your story go viral on your own, there are some steps you can take to make sure that it does. The worst thing the media can do is to ignore your campaign. This is even worse than them you attacking you. When they keep you out of the debates through corruption like Iowa Public Television did to several of my fellow candidates and me in Iowa, we responded. The response appears to have had a very negative impact on them financially. Hopefully, they learned their lesson, but I doubt it. It took a Libertarian candidate in Iowa dying for them to mention his name. The good news is that more people are starting to rely on social media and alternative media, and the power of the traditional media has severely deteriorated over the past few years.

While big media may include you or may give you the same treatment we received in Iowa, there are ways to occasionally break through a corrupt media without dying. There are several radio stations, local newspapers, and local TV news stations that will give you coverage even if the big ones do not. These are good practice. Several local papers don't have a lot of news to report. There have been third party candidates who get covered just by showing up in town and talking to the local newspaper editor or a reporter. In a previous chapter, I advised that the state party pay for a media list and have someone maintain it. The state party should also help candidates send out press releases.

If you want to get media coverage you need to think like a reporter. Like most of us, they are very busy. Their staff levels in most areas of the country have been severely cut. If you send them nonsense stories they are going to start to delete your e-mails before they read them. The key questions to ask before sending a press release are as follows:

- Is it newsworthy? Your opinions are not considered newsworthy. Responding to news stories, scandals, and announcing a campaign or major events are newsworthy.

- Is it timely? Are you responding to something that has recently happened or will happen in the near future?

- Is it written as a news story would appear in a newspaper? Don't add your own thoughts and opinions into the story. Write it so that a newspaper could copy and paste it into their paper and website without any editing. Many reporters are busy and will do this. Anytime you give an opinion, put quotes around it.

- Does it fit the audience? Do not take the easy way and send a blast e-mail to all media contacts. This is spam. Reporters hate it. If it is for a local event in St. Louis, someone in Springfield or Kansas City could care less.

In the appendix, I have attached two press releases that got me a lot of coverage. You begin with the "for immediate release" information, add a date, and a city. You end with the -30- mark and then place your contact information below. A press release should be brief, but able to get your main points across. The longer the story, the less likely it will be printed.

In addition to press releases, some newspapers will publish op-eds. Op-eds are simply opinion pieces which are about 300-500 words, and serve to make a case for or against an issue. Most papers will not take op-eds from candidates who have announced they are running for office, but will occasionally take letters to the editor and op-eds from libertarians. Tom Knapp has been publishing libertarian-leaning op-eds to newspapers across the world for years and has had great success doing so. Op-eds are sent in with a similar format to press releases.

Handling radio and television is a little different. If you have a friendly radio host this is usually no problem. You just stay on message and continue to bring up the main points that you want the listening audience to hear throughout the conversation. A hostile radio interviewer will try to derail you from staying on message. They will intentionally try to get you to talk about things that they think will hurt us among their audience. For example, they may ask you a question about abortion and say "Are you pro-life or pro-choice? It is yes no answer." Of course, anyone who has passed a college-level debate or critical thinking class could tell you that it is not a yes or no answer. It requires an explanation. If you let them get away with boxing you into a corner, they will. Occasionally, you have to turn the questions back on the radio host when they try to attack you.

When answering questions from any reporter it is always important to speak in soundbites. Some reporters have a bad habit of taking long statements and breaking them down to a sentence that distorts what you were trying to so. For example, if you say something followed by the word "but," they may report everything said before the word "but" and change the meaning of your statement.

CHAPTER 11

ORGANIZING THE COUNTY PARTY

Chapter 11 - Organizing The County Party

Everything I discuss in the next chapters about organizing the national and state party mean absolutely nothing if we do not take the first logical step and create strong county organizations. We must realize that expecting to have a few members on the state party executive committee to do all the work isn't feasible and will lead to burnout and stretch your resources too thin. That is what we are currently doing and it is failing miserably. This is why we need local groups to do the heavy lifting for the Libertarian Party. The local groups are much better able to know what local issues are important, who to recruit, where to hold events, and what candidates to run, rather than allowing someone all the way across the state to dictate these decisions.

In the past, county-level organization was impossible on a large scale. We didn't have the supporters to organize at the county level in most parts of the country. Today, it is difficult, but possible. I am not naive enough to believe that we will achieve a county organization in each county in the country in the next few years. That is fine. I am not even certain if the major parties can claim to have an active county organization in every county in the country. That being said, it is a goal and the more county organizations we have, the better we will do in elections and the more change we will be able to make.

What does the county party do? The county party is responsible for recruiting local and state legislative candidates, fighting against bad local laws, doing good in the community, and helping statewide and Congressional candidates with their efforts in the county. The county party is where everything is accomplished.

How do we get the county organizations to form? This is the most difficult thing. Organizing libertarians is like herding cats, and while I don't claim to be an expert in herding cats, I have a lot of experience trying to do so. The state party, which I discuss in detail in the next chapter, must take the leadership role in forming the county party. When the county organizations form, then they take the role of doing most of the work like recruiting candidates, attending events, etc. The current methods of having a few people in the state party travel around like a gypsy to recruit local candidates and man booths at county fairs and be in parades doesn't work. In doing so, we run out of resources very fast in most states larger than Rhode Island.

How often should the county party meet? The county party should have an official meeting at least once a month in a public place. The meeting should be posted on the state party website page and the Facebook page. In addition to political meetings, people should form social groups that meet up weekly or every other week at a bar or coffee shop to build friendships and alliances. Meetup.com requires a charge to use its services, but it is a good way to organize meetups. As part of a shameless self-promotion, I have started a website, www.libertarianrally.com, that will eventually attempt to bring libertarians together into local groups.

How to Structure the County Party:

The county party should have a Chair, Vice-Chair, Treasurer, and Secretary and should not charge for membership. Membership should be free to everyone who is a registered Libertarian, and if your state does not allow Libertarian Party registration, it should use the state party membership list to determine who can vote for party officers. The reason is simple. We don't want to have three levels of membership for someone where they need to join and pay dues to the county, state, and national party. Anyone who is a member of the state party should be a member of the county party.

The county party should have an annual convention before the state party convention, and every other year should elect party officers. The annual convention is the time to set a budget and strategy for the next year. It is a time to look at what goals we will set and the races and local political issues on which we plan to focus our efforts. It is also the time to audit the finances of the party and make sure that money is being spent properly.

Forming The County Party:

The first meeting is the most difficult to get set up. The state party should help set up the first meeting. To form the county party, we need an organizer to set up the first meeting. The organizer should work with the state party to get brochures, a speaker, and have a mailing sent out to all registered Libertarians and party members in the county announcing the event. It is also not a bad idea to hold the event at a public place such as a library and advertise the event on Facebook and in the local newspapers.

The goal of the first event is to see who would be interested in forming a county party. You would need a few members to officially form. Sometimes, a county party will form right there at the first meeting and elect an interim Chair, Vice-Chair, Treasurer, and Secretary. Often, people will want to think about it. Contact information of those who may be interested in forming the county party should be taken and followed up in a couple of weeks with a second meeting, if the county party did not form after the first meeting, to elect officers and approve the county party constitution, platform, and bylaws.

As a note, many people like to fight over platform issues. I recommend adopting the platform of the former Boston Tea Party which keeps things simple and doesn't bog us down in endless future debates:

We support reducing the size, scope and power of government at all levels and on all issues, and are opposed to increasing the size, scope and power of government at any level, for any purpose.

Once the county party has officially formed, they need to apply for affiliate status from the state party. The state party should then vote to affiliate or not affiliate the county party with the state party.

After the party has formed, you should ask the state party if they have an insurance policy you can use for liability insurance to have a booth at county fairs. Most county fair boards require an insurance policy. If the state party does not have one and you cannot convince them to get one, you can buy these for often around $100 a year. After that, I would see about replacing the state party.

The county party also should have a bank account at a local bank and see about what paperwork needs to be filed with the Secretary of State's office or ethics boards if your state has one. Often they require the treasurer to file paperwork after a certain amount of money has been raised or spent in an election year. Each state has different requirements. There may also be requirements and limits on how much individuals can give, or what types of candidates the county party can legally support financially.

In the appendix, I have attached sample county bylaws of the Libertarian Party of Pottawattamie County which was largely based on Gene Cisewski's How to Organize a County Affiliate guide. They obviously would need to be adjusted to meet the needs of your specific county and follow state rules. Under a state party that follows the local organizations strategy, they should be able to help you with this.

Keeping The Party Going:

The county party must hold regular meetings if they are going to remain active. The county party must attend and have a booth at the county fair, be in parades, and work to recruit candidates to run for local and county office. The county party should also have a local place be the unofficial campaign headquarters in election years to receive, store, and act as a pick-up location for campaign yard signs.

In addition to this, the county party exists to do good in the community, build networks, recruit registered voters, recruit candidates, and impact public policy. Without a strong county party, there is no need for a state or national party.

CHAPTER 12

ORGANIZING THE STATE PARTY

Chapter 12 - Organizing the state party

When looking at how we build the local political machine, we need to organize a strong state party. Without a strong state party, county affiliates will quickly die or more likely never get off the ground. Each state is going to have their board of directors organized slightly differently, so we make a few assumptions here. Some states may need to revise and update their Constitution and Bylaws so it doesn't hinder organization. For example, our state party Constitution and Bylaws should allow us to appoint volunteers to do main functions of the state party.

What functions should the state party be involved in? The state party is responsible for helping the county parties form and to affiliate them. It is responsible for recruiting candidates, building membership, increasing registered voters (if your state allows Libertarian voter registration), helping candidates get on the ballot, communicating with party members, and involvement in advertising and public relations.

The state party must have a board of directors, often called an executive committee, to set the goals and follow through with the agenda. As previously noted, the board of directors may not be organized in the exact same way for each state. There is also a debate over what the board of directors should do. Is it their job to just fundraise, should they only oversee the organization, should the board of directors run for office themselves? All of these are important questions we will take a look at.

We have to realize that we don't have a strong organization with thousands of party members in each state. That means that everyone has to do a larger share of work. This can lead to burnout. The key is to constantly recruit new activists and volunteers. Recruiting members and registered voters is great, but to avoid burnout and develop a strong organization, we must mentor the new leaders of the party. Additionally, we must never allow one person to have control over the party and do all the work. For one, there is too much work for one person to do. Another major issue with this strategy is that people burn out, get sick, and one day we all will pass away and we don't know when any of these things may happen. That is why we must always be recruiting, delegating, and mentoring the next leaders of the party. We will go into more details about how to recruit, delegate, and mentor future leaders a little later in the book.

Being that we are limited on how many members we have at this time, some people may have to hold several positions. As we build the organization those people must be willing to hand over leadership positions to new activists. When I was a manager in retail the question I always asked was, "who can I find to take over my job?" That is the question we must ask. Below, I list some positions that each state party will want. Keep in mind that your state may be set up differently as far as the organizational structure, and that you can add volunteer positions as they are needed.

Executive Committee (Board of Directors):

The executive committee sets the strategy and goals of an organization. It is important to keep the executive committee diverse in opinions, religion, age, gender, race, sexual orientation, etc. We want to build a party where all people are welcome, so long as they believe in our Libertarian principles and do not use fraud or force to harm others. We need activists, business men and women, college students, people who have run for office, and current and former elected officials to serve on the executive committee. We need young people to be ready to take over as the older members age. We need people who have been in the party for a long while to point out potential issues that will come up during each election and warn of potential inner-party fights that can occur.

The executive committee should meet once a month over phone or web video and three or four times a year in person to discuss and vote on party business. If you cannot get an executive committee to show up to three or four in-person meetings a year or to hold a monthly conference call over the phone, you need a new executive committee.

Something is lost when the people on a board of directors rarely or never meet in person. Additionally, the executive committee should know each other well enough that the members are comfortable working with each other on an individual basis for special projects and things such as candidate recruitment.

Party factions are natural and will often occur within any organization. This can lead to the party dividing and ultimately splitting up, which can destroy a state party. That is why it is critical to make sure the executive committee is made up of even-tempered individuals who don't aggressively fight or ridicule their fellow libertarians when they disagree. Executive committee members must be able to find common ground and work together. Additionally, they must be responsive to their membership and be willing to put in the time commitment to their position. The only thing worse than having a vacant position on a board of directors is having someone sabotaging your organization with a negative attitude, or someone who is not doing any work. To avoid burnout, committee members should serve terms and occasionally take terms off the committee when we get to a point where we have enough willing and qualified members to serve in these positions.

The executive committee should never become more concerned with parliamentary procedures than doing actual work. If you notice someone who is making power moves for executive committee positions to get their way and using parliamentary procedure to stifle productivity, it is time for the membership to remove that member during the next time they elect their executive committee at their state convention. Unfortunately, some people want to be a big fish in a small pond and do not like to hand over power, no matter how small that power may be. Below, we look at positions that serve on the executive committee, what they do, and the type of person you want to have serve in that position:

The Chair:

The state party Chair is the leader of the state party. Think of him or her as the Chief Executive Officer of a corporation. They should have the power to appoint all volunteer positions, which we will talk about a little later, upon approval from the executive committee. He or she should be someone that is good with working with others and not a vocal member of any party factions.

The state party Chair should have experience working within other organization and within the Libertarian Party and should have served at least a term on the executive committee before being elected as chair. They should be a known leader within the party and while people have different strengths, and a great candidate might not make a good state party chair and a good state party chair might not make a good candidate, it is not a bad idea to consider someone who has run for office before. Ideally, the state party chair should not run for office while serving, as the chair should spend his or her time recruiting and helping the other candidates and overseeing the state party organization; however, we are still a small organization and we desperately need candidates to run for office.

The party Chair should have a vision and goals for the state party. They must be able to run a fair meeting and have a basic understanding of Roberts Rules of Order. The state party Chair must support the local organization effort and must never run the party like a dictatorship or one in which they are unable to recruit or delegate. They should be able to articulate the libertarian message, look professional, and be willing to roll up their shirt sleeves and go to work wherever they are needed. The chair should be replaced by the party membership after a couple of terms in the position to avoid burnout and to give new ideas and people the ability to prosper.

The Vice-Chair:

The Vice-Chair, depending on the needs of the organization, could have a few different duties. They could help build the organization and develop county parties. They could recruit members and candidates, and identify possible people to fill executive committee positions that need filled. On the other hand, they could be someone the state party chair is mentoring to take over as state party chair. The Vice-Chair should be someone who, like the chair, every faction can work with and someone who is willing to lead the party and roll up their shirt sleeves and get to work. They must be able to take over as state party chair if the need ever arises. Previous state party chairs and new and upcoming members looking to take over as chair often make good vice-chairs.

Treasurer:

The Treasurer should be an honest and trustworthy person. They need to make sure that the party is in a strong financial position and warn the executive committee of any potential revenue issues they see with membership levels decreasing, ballot access, and convention expenses. The Treasurer is also responsible for filing state ethics committee reports on funds raised and expenses. An audit committee should ensure that the Treasurer is depositing all checks and that the Treasurer is being a good steward of the organization's assets by filing state ethics reports on time, since a failure to do can result in fines to the state party.

Secretary:

The Secretary is the person who keeps all the meeting minutes and makes sure that the meeting minutes are uploaded to the party website. We are not running a secret society and should not keep secrets from our party members. The minutes should give accurate notes of every motion made and seconded, as well as the vote results, and be approved by the executive committee at the next meeting. Once again, the audit committee should oversee this to make sure the minutes are being accurately published in a timely manner. The meeting minutes are not the place for a lot of extra notes and lengthy comments. Doing so can put the party at unnecessary risk for potential litigation.

Congressional District Representatives:

Many states will elect their executive committee representatives by Congressional district. Each district representative should help organize all the county organizations within their district, as well as work with affiliates in their district. The district representatives should work to recruit a congressional district candidate as well as with the county organizations to recruit local candidates. Additionally, they should organize one major event in their district each year.

At-Large Representatives:

As Kevin Litten, who was a longtime activist in Iowa, would say, no one on the executive committee should have nothing to do. If you can give an at-large representative something to do, that is the best thing to do. Personally, I am in favor of having the at-large representatives help recruit statewide candidates and oversee ballot access.

Other Positions:

Your state may have other positions such as director of campaigns and elections, director of membership, and director of advocacy and public policy. I am of the belief that these positions should be eliminated. The reason is that these are very important positions, and when you get someone in those positions who isn't doing their job, you have to wait up to two years to replace them at the next executive committee election. The Constitution and Bylaws of the state party should be revised to move these positions under the volunteer staff positions which we will mention later.

Audit Committee and Judicial Committee:

The audit committee and judicial committees are critical in protecting the organization. Hopefully, the judicial committee is never needed. It makes the decisions on any power struggles within the party. The audit committee is to be used every year. The job of the audit committee is to look for any discrepancies in financial records, as well as potential future issues such as not having one person owning the website domain or having one person with all the website codes. A good example of this happened with the Iowa Republican Party. When they lost a staffer who had all the website passwords they couldn't update their website or social media for approximately a month. Neither one should have anyone on it that is part of the executive committee or is accepting money from the party.

Staff:

Now, we talk about something different than most states have ever done and that is to create volunteer staff positions that are under the control and direction of the state chair and approved by the executive committee. Your state may have different positions than those which we list below, and some positions may not be necessary or be able to be filled at this point. The vacant positions can be listed on the state party website and volunteers can sign up to be considered for them.

Executive Director:

We are going to make an assumption that most states are not at a point where they need an executive director and that position is largely going to be filled by the state chair; however, as the organization grows and develops the state chair may have enough work that they find they need an executive director to carry out many of their goals and objectives. At the point that an executive director is needed, their functions would be similar to that of the state chair. This position, at some point in the future, will likely become a paid position, but most states are a little ways off from that just yet.

Communications Director:

The communications director distributes press releases to media, updates social media such as Twitter and Facebook, updates the website, and delivers talking points to candidates. The communications director is also responsible for sending out the newsletter to party members and helping with advertising the party and candidates. The state party must be very careful to make sure they have a review committee to look over and review communications that come from the state party to make certain they adhere to our beliefs and they are professional written.

Outreach (Volunteer) Coordinator

The outreach or volunteer coordinator is responsible for making sure that every volunteer is responded to and put in contact with their local group. The volunteer coordinator is responsible for establishing and strengthening the county organizations.

Director of Campaigns and Elections:

I mentioned this position before, as it is often part of the executive committee. This position should be moved to the volunteer staff, as it gives more control over the executive committee to ensure that the tasks related to this position are done.

Should we have an office?

Now that we have looked at what positions the state party should have, we ask ourselves if we should have a physical office. I am going to give you the politician's answer of both yes and no. There are arguments for and against having an office and then there are practical implications such as the important question of whether we are ready to have an office. Each state will be different, but below we address some of those questions.

The argument against having an office is simple. We live in a world of instant online communications where most functions can be done remotely by individuals across the state. This means that staff don't need to show up and meet in person and that you spread out your staff across the state, which is beneficial for a small party that often doesn't have a core group of people located in one area that could run the state party office.

Of course, there is a counterargument to not having an office. The state party needs to store records, and in many cities, office space is very cheap, and a central location at a small office can allow volunteers a place to go to make phone calls, print brochures, and stamp envelopes.

At some point, as the party grows, even with the move toward more online communications, I cannot anticipate an organization not having an office. It can save money by having a central location to ship campaign materials to and for volunteers and candidates to meet without having to meet in a public place where opponents may eavesdrop on our campaign plans. The question is when you spend money on an office. The questions to look at are below:

Would we use it?

How would we use it?

Do we have volunteers to maintain it?

Can we financially afford it?

If we fund the office space, what are we not funding?

When you are able to afford an office and you identify that you need one, you should look for one centrally located or near a large base of volunteers. Please note that college towns are often good choices, except that during the summer campaign many college students are out of town.

Advice For The State Party:

"We must all hang together, or assuredly we shall all hang separately." Ben Franklin

In the previous chapter I briefly gave some limited advice for the state party. This chapter expands upon how to run the organization once the leadership and the volunteer state party staff is in place. As we grow, party factions will occur. Personality conflicts will appear. In fact, some states may split, join others parties, etc. Other states may suffer from fringe candidates, fraud, bad leaders, and even face a hostile takeover. County parties face the same issues; however, it is a lot easier to fix a bad county party than an entire state organization. This chapter exists to help the strong state party stay together.

All it takes is one bad state party chair with one term, a corrupt treasurer or executive director with little oversight, or one really bad idea, no matter how well intentioned, to destroy a good state party. This often happens because we don't have experienced people on the executive committees or we get lazy in our duties. The executive committee is a volunteer position and many libertarians, especially considering that most of our members are under 35 years old, get very busy with early career and family obligations. We need to be able to quickly replace executive committee members when they need to temporarily step down. This is not possible until we have a strong organization with a lot of people who have business and political experience and are able to serve on the executive committee board.

Before we look at an external hostile takeover of a state party, we should look at a more likely scenario: the bad leader. The bad leader may or may not have the party's best interest at hand. He or she may not have had a great amount of leadership experience. They may have personality traits that don't work well with others. They may not know how to organize. They may also be running a corrupt scam to embezzle money. Regardless of whether it is incompetence or a Trojan horse, the results of bad leadership will destroy a state party.

There are two qualities to stay away from when electing party leaders. The first is a person who is very negative and the second is a person who is overly positive. Both will burn out an organization and one may be trying to get rich. Sounds kind of like a contradiction, doesn't it?

An overly negative leader is not one that inspires confidence and a reason to join the party. They miss key opportunities and always find the negative. Positive thinking is key. No one wants to join a party full of losers. Here is an example: ask someone out on a date and be like the late Chris Farley playing Matt Foley, the motivational speaker on Saturday Night Live and say "I'm 35 years old. I am divorced. I live in a van down by the river." See where that gets you. Don't be a party full of losers. Elect party leaders who have a vision, a little charisma, and a positive attitude.

So we don't want a negative person, but how about an overly positive person? A positive person is good to have for the reasons mentioned in the paragraph above; however, the Libertarian Party has a real problem with leaders and candidates that have burned hard working activists out because of promises of election results that did not happen because the groundwork had never been laid. More important, one of the reasons the groundwork wasn't laid was because many libertarians were expecting a miracle while we were sitting on our asses waiting for someone else to make it happen. We need men and women in leadership who are positive, but also realistic, and who realize that creating a gold state doesn't happen in one or two elections. It is a fight that will take years and even decades. Celebrate small victories and keep pushing forward. Dream the impossible dream, but don't for one second think we are going to get there overnight without doing any real work.

The third thing to watch for in a bad leader ties to the positive leader. This is the leader that is very positive about a new "get successful quick" scheme that they have devised. This person may or may not be well meaning. Often, they have a scam to recruit a celebrity candidate or get "Ron Paul to run as a Libertarian" and think that all of our issues will be resolved. When that fails, we are back where we were. Here is another secret. I've received over 60,000 votes in 2 statewide Iowa elections. Ron Paul has received a little over 40,000. Even if everyone who supported him didn't vote for me, I would still be under 5%. Having all his supporters join, no matter the benefit, still doesn't win us elections.

The other possibility is that the leader with this "get successful quick" scheme is trying to run a scam or may really believe in their own product, and will design an app, phone banking software, or web design software that will "win us elections" while costing the party a ton of money. This is how the Libertarian Party can very quickly go bankrupt on poorly coded or designed products.

The leaders who refuse to give up power and are unable to delegate present another issue. Two terms as state party chair is really enough for anyone to serve consecutively. Even a very good chair will burn out or lose great ideas or the ability to see the organization without severe tunnel vision. In the past, we had a very small organization and this couldn't always be avoided. In some states with a weak or non-existent state party, this may very well be an issue that you will face.

How do you stop embezzlement in the state party and protect our finances and resources? One of the real benefits of the *Gold State Plan* is that it doesn't leave a lot of money to be kept in the state party bank account. With local organization, we aren't spending much money from the state party bank account. Instead, we are focused on spending our resources at the local level. That means that we aren't spending money from the top down on things that may or may not work in certain local areas. It also means that there is not much money that can be lost due to embezzlement or lawsuits. Additionally, the *Gold State Plan* calls for an audit committee to audit all finances yearly, and have multiple people listed on the bank account, and the executive committee should compare the bank statements with the treasurer's report once a month before the monthly meeting.

The party chair, with the advice of the executive committee, sets a series of goals for their term. These goals include membership numbers, number of candidates, and goals with regards to how many county organizations are active and vote results. The goals should be S.M.A.R.T goals, meaning they should be:

Specific

Measurable (how much)

Assignable (able to be delegated to someone or a group)

Realistic ("anarchy next Tuesday" is not realistic)

Time-based (by when)

County organizations will also want to set their own goals and each state and county party will have different goals based on their strengths, weaknesses, and opportunities that are specific to their state.

Another area the state party is responsible for is the state party website and all social media pages. As a security measure, the state party should always own the domain and have a party bank account attached to the domain and hosting. I have several Stephen King-style horror stories about state parties, even the Iowa Republican Party, and candidates who lost access to their domain or website login information. Losing access to a website or social media page looks unprofessional and could allow something controversial to be posted.

Each state party should have a few people who can do a rapid response to news; however, this person should have experience in dealing with the media and dealing with crisis situations. We had two crisis situations in 2014 in Iowa. In one, a candidate passed away. In another, a candidate was charged with sexual assault. Both were nationwide stories and we handled both very well. Either one could have easily been a disaster for PR depending on how we handled it. It is difficult to lose a friend and then get a series of calls from reporters that you don't like who refused to cover you in the past. Likewise, it is difficult when you know criminal charges against your candidate are false, but won't be dismissed until after an election. In this case, you have to say something without saying actually saying anything and without saying the words "no comment," as it looks terrible. Likewise, you need someone who knows how to push the controversy line just far enough to get post views and media views, but not to take it too far. 9/11 truth, reposting racist memes, Republican talking points, or favorable news about candidates of other parties, (I had a county Democrat party post favorable things about my campaign on Facebook once) and various anti-vaccination and conspiracy theories quickly take us off message and do great harm.

One of the best features to use on Facebook is the advertising feature. You can boost important stories and promote the Facebook page. You target libertarians in your state and you get them to like the page and then you have a dedicated group to share your content to a wide audience and attend your local events. The state party will coordinate with the county parties on promoting good things going on in their communities and local candidates. In addition to finding someone who can handle PR well, you also want to find someone who can create memes for each of the local candidates.

The website should have a blog that is updated at least once a week, a volunteer and contact form, separate login and pages for each county party to have their own page, a short biography and photo of each candidate, copies of historical voting statistics with records listed, names of previous state chairs, previous meeting minutes, and links to the social media pages. The volunteer page should list the volunteer positions that were listed in the previous chapter.

The national party is responsible for hosting a national convention every other year and the state party is responsible for hosting a state party convention once every year or two. I recommend once a year as it is a great networking opportunity for libertarians in the state and, if done correctly, it can make money for the state party. Each state is different, but high population areas in the center of the state are often good for large geographical states. The convention shouldn't last too long and it should have multiple opportunities for people to network. At least one keynote speaker should be invited.

The convention is also where a hostile takeover of the state party would occur. If your state does not have a primary and nominates candidates at the convention you could have a hostile takeover by packing the convention to replace the dedicated and actual libertarians who plan to run. Another possibility is that they overthrow your executive committee. That is why it is a good idea to have an annual convention where the candidates and executive committee are decided in different years. This prevents a complete takeover of the state party at one convention.

One way to prevent a hostile takeover is to have the state party bylaws require that voting members be members and registered Libertarians (if your state allows) at least one month before the convention. The membership requirement for people just signing up can and should be waived by the current members if it is determined that this is not a possibility at the start of the convention. That being said, the best way to prevent a hostile takeover is to build such a large organization that it is very difficult and expensive for a non-libertarian individual or group to try to take over the party. As the party grows, expect non-libertarians to try to cause problems. This also happened in Costa Rica, where they had someone get elected as a Libertarian who was not really a Libertarian and left the party, costing them a seat.

Another method to preventing a hostile takeover of the state party is to not allow your executive committee to endorse or work for a candidate of another party or register to vote as a member of another party. Critics will come in and say this Republican or Democrat candidate is the new Messiah and they are your "only hope to win" and that you need to help them and without your help they won't win. Pardon my language, but I've heard this bullshit before. There is no "get successful quick" scheme that will transform us into a libertarian country and that includes the Presidential race for the major parties. Even if you elect a libertarian President, you still don't have a libertarian country. Likewise, the Libertarian Party is not large enough to influence a Republican or Democrat primary. Additionally, how offensive would it be if we demanded another party support our candidates? We would be laughed out of the room. By using party resources on a candidate of another party we open ourselves to future issues and an eventual hostile takeover where Republicans or Democrats hijack our party and nominate their own candidates who will be as libertarian as Lyndon Johnson or Richard Nixon were.

If your candidates are nominated by a state primary you have fewer options. I know several of you may remember a fringe candidate in Missouri that continued to win in a primary and embarrass the party. That is why we need to run good libertarians for every office possible, and organize and explain to our members the importance of voting in the Libertarian primary and not the two major parties. Once again, if registered Libertarians do their job we won't nominate embarrassing candidates for high office very often.

In addition to the bank accounts and website information being secured, all party historical records should be kept in a safe area where they will not be destroyed or stolen. I could tell several stories about this happening within the Libertarian Party as well, and while it doesn't have the same impact as someone stealing login information to the website or social media, it does harm the institutional memory necessary in building a long-term political organization.

How does the state party grow membership and increase registered voters? The *Gold State Plan* doesn't require a lot of members to run an organization; however, we do need to have several members who show up at the conventions, serve on committees, and handle the business of the state party. The state party should use the statewide and federal campaigns in its state to try and get people to join the party. It should provide members with a monthly electronic newsletter and make the state convention something they want to become a member to attend. Likewise, county organizations that require members of the county party be registered Libertarians increases members, as does running a lot of good candidates. You will see the numbers explode almost overnight when you get a lot of strong county parties and strong local candidates.

Taking Over A Bad State Party:

Occasionally, you will find a state party that is either almost non-existent or that is in need of change and the current leadership blocks any change through parliamentary tricks or not calling meetings. Don't worry. The *Gold State Plan* has two methods to take over a bad state party that is blocking reform.

The best thing to do is to try to build coalitions with the state party leaders and win them over. Many times, people are frightened by change. If you have ever worked in management you are probably familiar with having to earn people's trust before they stop trying to sabotage you. Sometimes, new people can come across as very aggressive or condescending towards people who have dedicated a lot of time and financial resources to something.

If building coalitions and working with them doesn't work, the first method to try is to recruit a group of libertarians in your state,show up at the next convention and try to get new blood into the positions of officers. If the state is not holding meetings, you should contact your Representatives on the Libertarian National Committee and the national party staff. This is why we have a national party and I'm sure they would be more than happy to help. If they have a convention, make sure you are all registered libertarians, members of the state party, and understand the bylaws. Be well -organized and decide what positions you are going to run for well in advance.

What if that strategy doesn't work? We have another one. This requires you to form your own Political Action Committee (PAC). With the PAC, you can do many of the functions the state party should be doing but is not. You can likely recruit candidates, start county organizations, and lobby on legislative issues. Eventually, if the state party is not active, your PAC will become large enough to overtake the bad state party and corrupt the old boys club in the state party. The PAC can then dissolve and the work can be done by the new state party that supports local organization and political action.

THE ROLE OF THE NATIONAL PARTY AND PRESIDENTIAL CAMPAIGN

Chapter 13 - The Role of The National Party and Presidential Campaign

"If only we ran celebrity candidates for a former politician we will win national elections." Sorry to disappoint you, but Libertarians lose because we focus our limited resources on a nationwide top-down strategy without first building the local organization. Some Libertarians understand this and go to the other extreme, and believe that we shouldn't focus on the national party at all. The national party is critical in its support and development of state and local organizations, but it cannot replace them.

We often find that Libertarians, with quixotic efforts to take over the Republican Party, give up and claim that politics is a lost cause after one or two unsuccessful elections. We do not have the resources to win at the Presidential level. We don't have the organization, the money, the staff, the time, or the structure in place from previous campaigns. I am a big fan of positive thinking, but it is foolish to get peoples' hopes up and lie to them about our chances. It is similar to the "get rich easy and quick" schemes that many fraudulent multi-level marketers user. There is no replacement for local organization, and running a good Presidential campaign takes years of hard work and local groups.

I've been to events put on by Presidential candidates from the major parties. Trust me, their candidates and their staff are often not much more organized than many of our Libertarian Party candidates; however, they have a mailing list and local groups they can call upon to get a group of people to show up at their events. That is why someone running for President as a Democrat or Republican can fly into Iowa City, Iowa and speak to a crowd of over 100 people on a short notice. When I ran for Secretary of State in 2014, I traveled the state and often spoke to groups much larger than some of the other statewide candidates for the major parties; however, when they needed a crowd they had a list they could call on and while I had a list, it was a fraction of the size of their list.

A question many Libertarians have asked is whether we should even run a Presidential nominee. The idea is that it takes resources from local candidates and puts the focus on an unwinnable race. The truth is that resources are not scarce. Our Presidential nominees raise about 1-2 million dollars on average. Even if everyone who donated made the choice to instead donate that money and spread it out across the country, it wouldn't produce magical results. Additionally, how many of you reading this came into the Libertarian Party because of a Presidential campaign? I came into the party after watching Gary Nolan, who ran unsuccessfully for the Libertarian Party Presidential nomination in 2004 on TV and became a Libertarian Party supporter during Badnarik's Presidential campaign. Many old timers (I know I will be criticized for calling you that) came to the party during the Harry Browne 1996 campaign and some of the really old timers campaigned for Ed Clark all the way back in 1980 which, I might add, was 8 years before I was even born. Many of us would never have heard of the Libertarian Party without the party running a Presidential campaign. Real, real old timers like Tim Hird, the state party Treasurer in Iowa, have been around since the 70's.

The Presidential race is the only race on which many Americans focus. It is an opportunity for almost every voter in the country, with the exception of Oklahoma where it is next to impossible for us to get on the ballot, to vote for a Libertarian candidate. It allows for the coverage of several libertarian issues and gives us great media mentions. The Presidential race is also critical for some states to achieve ballot access. For example, in Iowa, once we become a major party, we will need to run a Presidential candidate every four years to maintain major party status.

Running a Presidential campaign is necessary for the local organizations strategy and not running a Presidential candidate would destroy the Libertarian Party. If the Presidential campaign is properly run, it is a great benefit for the party and local organization. It strengthens local organizations, recruits members to both the state and national party, and provides organizational support to weak statewide organizations.

What should we look for in a Presidential nominee? The Presidential nominee should not be a charlatan who espouses libertarian ideas only to gain our nomination. We should look for individuals who have organizational strengths, name recognition, charisma, who support libertarian stands on the issues, and who have had a history of activism within our party. The stronger our local organizations are, the better choices we will have for our Presidential nominees. It looks bad when we only nominate former Republicans who have previously lost races as Republicans and now want to join the party and then leave a year or two after running for our highest office.

How should the Presidential campaign be run? It is a real tragedy that two of our last Presidential candidates ran their campaigns by racking up over a million dollars in debt and not paying their bills. In fact, former Congressman Bob Barr, our 2008 Presidential nominee, was sued for allegedly not paying his ghostwriter Jim Bovard $47,000 after his campaign ended. This is not how to run a campaign. It is also not a good idea to pay extremely high salaries to staff when you are running on approximately a million dollar budget for a national campaign. I'm not here to attack Governor Johnson or Congressman Barr. People often complain about libertarians airing all of our dirty laundry in public, but if the delegates to our national conventions did their laundry a little more often, it wouldn't be dirty and therefore it wouldn't be aired.

A good Presidential campaign will have a coordinator in every state and one in the District of Columbia. Ideally, they would also have one in each territory like Puerto Rico; although those votes are non-binding they deserve local libertarian government just like the rest of us. A good campaign will distribute yard signs, try to get the candidate to each state, use their campaign to help endorse and recruit local candidates, give several TV and radio interviews, and provide support to struggling state party organizations by getting their volunteers to help with more local campaigns and getting some of those volunteers active within the state party leadership.

You can read an article I wrote in 2008 on the successes and failures of the Barr Presidential campaign in the appendix.

Now that we have discussed why we need to run a Presidential campaign, what type of candidate we should run, and how the campaign should run to promote the local organization, we will discuss the national party in detail.

The national party is a very small part of the organization. It operates on a shoestring budget. You may think this is a bad thing. It is and it isn't a bad thing. We want a small national staff to keep the focus on a decentralized, bottom-up, and not top-down organization. Large numbers of staffers also can lead to larger corruption and scandals. That being said, the current situation in the national party is good. We have a good staff, a great Executive Director, Wes Benedict, and a great national Chairman, Nicholas Sarwark, but long-term we need to correct a few errors that could greatly harm the national party.

It is a bad sign that membership in the Libertarian Party remains stagnant at about 14,000 total members despite the fact that our candidates are receiving higher vote totals and percentages, and are breaking Libertarian Party records. Additionally, there are more registered Libertarian Party voters than ever before. Add in the fact that membership has remained at the same level of $25 for years and inflation has gone up and you quickly realize that we have a serious problem.

Once upon a time, about 15 years ago, a few years before I became involved in the Libertarian Party, we had a program called the Unified Membership Plan (UMP). The UMP made all members of the state party organizations national party members. The state parties would then receive a percentage of money for the membership. Critics called it welfare for weak state parties and said it relied too heavily on membership recruitment at the expense of building the local organization. The transition away from the UMP caused a severe crisis in several state party organizations when they no longer were receiving money from the national party and had to start their own membership recruitment strategy.

Today, membership at the state and national party are separate. Each state organization decides, based on their own needs, who is a member in the state party and how much, if anything, membership should cost. Some states even have different levels of membership. Membership for the state and local organizations were discussed earlier in the book; however, we will look at how we can increase membership in the national party in this chapter.

As a party, we are not going back to the UMP plan. Changing our membership back and forth can lead to major disasters in organizational strength. With that being said, we must ask how we can increase membership under the model we are currently using, why people are not becoming members, whether we should increase membership dues, and what benefits members receive.

The national party needs funding, so should we increase membership dues? Should we keep dues at the same $25? How do we increase national party membership? These are not easy questions to answer. Obviously if dues remain at the same level, the state party has less money each year from the same dues when normal inflation rates of 2-3% are factored in. On the other hand, if membership is stagnant, which it is, how do we increase membership by charging more? There are a few factors that we must consider.

One of the major hindrances is that a very large percentage of libertarians fall into the millennial generation of young voters born since the early 1980's. I am in this category. This age group is largely libertarian because the Democrats and Republicans have really screwed them. Just look at the massive national debt and unfunded liabilities, and then factor in the fact that big businesses use government regulations to screw employees and churn the workforce to keep wages low and increase short-term profit. Not to mention the student loan bubble that has put millions of young people into debt in a bad economy where they can't find work that pays the bills. That is before we even mention the wars. While these factors have caused more young people to discover libertarianism, these same factors keep young libertarians poor. While I am a few years older now and have done well financially, when I was a younger libertarian, $50 for annual membership dues plus fees to attend conventions and state party and local membership would have been a lot of money. That being said, young libertarians will donate money to worthwhile causes.

What types of things excite young people enough to part with their hard-earned money to become a card-carrying Libertarian Party member? We don't have to look far. A lot of young people gave a lot of money to Ron Paul's 2008 and 2012 Presidential campaigns. The reason they donated and became part of a movement was momentum. No one wants to join a loser. When you are making noise and having some success, people will join. Unfortunately, while we are having a lot of recent success getting our libertarian ideas such as government out of marriage and ending marijuana prohibition implemented, we have failed to show people that we are winning. When people continue to see our candidates receive 2-3% they don't view that as a victory even if our opponents implement every idea of ours in an attempt to gain back those people who voted for Libertarian candidates. Until we explain this strategy and start to focus on winnable races, those young libertarians will continue to follow the Pied Piper into the GOP.

Now that we have gone through the *Gold State Plan*, it is time to get to work!

Draft By-Laws Constitution and Platform:

PLATFORM

The Libertarian Party of Pottawattamie County supports reducing the size, scope and power of government at all levels and opposes increasing the size, scope and power of government at any level for any purpose.

CONSTITUTION

Libertarian Party of Pottawattamie County

Article I Name

The name of this organization shall be "The Libertarian Party of Pottawattamie County."

Article II Purpose

The purpose of this organization shall be to advance, in every honorable way, fundamental Libertarian principles and policies. As a voluntary organization, we shall cooperate and assist in all city, county, state, and national elections to the end that our Constitutional form of limited government for the United States and our state be preserved for all of the people.

As a part of the Libertarian state voluntary organization, this organization shall direct, manage, supervise and control the business and the funds of the Libertarian Party of Pottawattamie County.

Article III Membership

Membership in this organization shall be open to all Pottawattamie County citizens who are current registered members of the Libertarian Party.

Qualified and voting members of this organization shall be those Libertarians in good standing who have been recorded by the Secretary/Treasure of this organization for at least 30 days prior to any meeting.

Article IV Officers and Executive Committee

Section 1: The officers of this organization shall consist of a Chair, a First Vice Chair, a Secretary, and a Treasurer, and such other officers as shall be provided for in the bylaws.

Section 2: Duties of the Officers
The chair shall preside at all meetings or caucuses of the party and of the executive

committee, and shall have general supervision of the work of the organization.

The vice chair, in the absence of the chair, shall perform the duties of the chair (as outlined in the bylaws).

The secretary shall keep and read minutes of meetings or caucuses and shall promptly issue membership cards to all qualifying members.

The treasurer shall receive and be custodian of all funds of the party and shall pay all bills. The treasurer shall keep an account of all monies received and disbursed and shall report in full, as required by the chair, to the executive committee. The treasurer shall file all proper reports as required by law.

Section 3: The term of office for the officers and executive committee shall be two years, and until their successors are elected and installed in every odd number year. The first officers' term will be up at the 2015 convention.

Section 4: All officers and members of the executive committee shall be elected in a duly constituted county caucus or meeting.

Section 5: The executive committee shall be made up of the officers and those additional individuals as set forth in the bylaws.

Article V Meetings, Caucuses

Section 1: Meetings or caucuses shall be held under proper notice, at the call of the chair.

Section 2: A regular county meeting or caucus shall be held each year, at which time delegates and alternates shall be elected to attend the congressional district caucus and the state convention, and for the election of officers as needed under state law.

Section 3: The executive committee shall hold meetings at such times as are determined by the executive committee.

Section 4: Special meetings of the executive committee may be called by the chair or by written request of two members of the executive committee, and upon notice to all members.

Section 5: A county meeting or caucus shall be called and advertised online at the state party website at least ten days prior to said meeting, and in a direct mailing to all registered Libertarians in the county.

Section 6: Voting by proxy shall be prohibited at any regular or special county meeting or caucus.

Article VI Nominations and Elections

Section 1: A nominating committee of not less than five members shall be appointed by the chair and approved by the executive committee prior to each election. This committee shall report one nominee for each office at the meeting/caucus for such election after which nominations from the floor shall be allowed. (If required by state law)

Section 2: A nominating committee of not less than three members shall be appointed by the chair and approved by the executive committee for the purpose of nominating delegates and alternates to attend each state convention and district caucus after which nominations may be made from the floor. (If required by state law)

Section 3: Where there is only one candidate for an office, election may be by voice.

Section 4: Where more than one candidate is nominated for an office, election will be by written ballot. A majority of votes cast shall elect.

Article VII Appointments

All recommendations for appointments shall be made by the chair, with the approval of a majority of the executive committee.

Article VIII Quorum

Section 1: A quorum for a meeting or caucus of the organization shall be a majority of the members present.

Section 2: A quorum for a meeting of the executive committee shall be a majority of the executive committee.

APPENDIX

Article IX Parliamentary Authority

Roberts' Rules of Order, Newly Revised, shall govern all proceedings except where inconsistent with the Constitution and bylaws of this organization.

Article X Bylaws

Bylaws may be adopted in compliance with this constitution by a majority vote at any duly called county meeting or caucus.

Article XI Conflict

In the event of any conflict or ambiguity of the constitution or bylaws adopted hereunder, the constitution of the Libertarian Party of Iowa shall prevail.

Article XII Amendments

Amendments to the constitution may be made after approved by the state executive committee and by a two-thirds vote at any regular or special meeting or caucus of this organization where the call and notice states such purpose.

A Model For Libertarian Influence In Iowa
By Jake Porter
April 2, 2015

On April 19th, the Libertarian Party of Iowa will celebrate its 40th anniversary. We have had more success in the past year than we have ever had as far as vote totals and percentages are concerned. The success was demonstrated at our annual convention last Saturday. That being said, we have been wandering in the political desert for 40 years just like Israelites and we are in search of our own Moses to lead us to the Promised Land, which brings me to the Costa Rica model for the Libertarian Party of Iowa.

In May of 1994, Otto Guevara founded the Partido Movimiento Libertario (Libertarian Movement Party in English) of Costa Rica as an alternative to the political organizations in the country. Of course, Costa Rica has a multi-party system which makes things a lot easier than they have been in Iowa, and so the methods are not the same, but the ideas of how to influence our state legislature are. The major difference is that in Costa Rica it is not a winner-take-all system like we have.

In 1998, Guevara was elected to the legislature and spent considerable time improving his skills, and by being elected was able to use the media to influence the debate, which his think tank involvement had been unable to do. Guevara told Reason Magazine in 2003, "I'm convinced that political participation is a much more effective way of promoting freedom than any 10 books you could write." The party had the same issues that we have with the media, but when they started electing Libertarians the issue was resolved.

Guevara ran for President in 2002 and received under 2% of the vote, but elected 6 of the 57 legislators. He ran again in 2006 and the party and received under 10%, and in 2010 he ran and received 20% of the vote and almost won the election. Today, they still have 4 out of 57 seats in the legislature.

In Iowa, we need to do the same thing that the Partido Movimeiento Libertario did in Costa Rica. We need to run as many professional candidates as we possibly can for the state legislature. 53% of all state legislative races were uncontested in 2014. Think of how many members of the state legislature get arrested or are involved in a major scandal each year. If the Libertarian Party of Iowa runs someone for every race, we are going to win a seat in the state legislature. When that happens, the media will be forced to pay attention to us and not wait for one of us to die in a plane crash while campaigning or to be charged with sexual assault.

In 2016, we need to run as many good candidates as possible and by doing so we will find our Moses along the way and we will be led out of the political desert.

The Successes and Failures of the Barr Campaign:
By Jake Porter
May 1, 2009

Shortly after the Bob Barr 2008 Presidential campaign ended, I received many questions regarding both the successes and failures of the campaign. After all, I was an early opponent of Bob Barr, I was in Kansas City, Missouri when Bob announced his exploratory committee, and I was in Denver when he finally won the nomination. In fact, Bob received my delegate vote every round after George Phillies was defeated. In my humble opinion, Bob Barr is a very good man and he had the best intentions of the Libertarian Party in mind when running. In this article, I will try to present both the successes and failures of the campaign in a non-confrontational or condemning manner.

A day after Bob won the nomination, I phoned someone involved with the campaign to volunteer and had to leave a message on their voicemail. Unfortunately, I never heard back from this person. After I flew back from Denver, I e-mailed a campaign staffer asking to volunteer. Remember, I was not asking for a paying job. Attached was my resume, which includes managing campaigns and other large groups as well as being elected Alternate to a

Region of the Libertarian National Committee, and while I am very young, my political experience is nothing to be completely scoffed at. This time, I was informed it would be put at the top of the to-do list. Once again, I never heard anything back in response to volunteering. A week or so later, I was informed that Mike Ferguson was named my Regional Coordinator for the Barr campaign. Mike is a very competent political campaigner who has been elected to public office. I e-mailed Mike and within hours received a phone call from him. In my experience with volunteers, many would have given up after the first or second attempt to try to volunteer.

Around the middle of July, I was named Iowa Coordinator for the campaign. This allowed me to see firsthand both the successes and failures of the Barr campaign. It is my hope that by releasing this article, in the future, we can improve upon our successes and not repeat the failures. It is not, nor has it ever been, my intention to attack anyone for trying an idea that didn't work. As the quote that I have posted on my desk by Theodore Roosevelt goes, "The credit belongs to the man who is actually in the arena, whose face is marred by dust and sweat and blood, who strives valiantly, who errs and comes up short again and again, because there is no effort without error or shortcoming."

Success and Failures:

Advertising:

In 2004, I actually remember seeing a couple of the Michael Badnarik television ads on CNN Headline News. In 2008, I saw and heard no Bob Barr advertisements. The video ad of 2008, in my opinion, was less visually appealing than the 2004 television ad I had seen of Michael Badnarik. I have no idea if the Barr campaign used any television or radio advertising either nationwide or statewide. I know they had a couple of radio ads produced and at least one ad that could have been used on television, but I have no evidence that they ever ran. If they did, there was certainly not much of an attempt to promote the fact that they were running. Many times the fact that you are running ads is worth more in media attention than the advertisements themselves.

Additionally, I asked to fundraise in Iowa for our own advertising. All my polling and sources strongly indicated to me that Obama was going to win Iowa by a large vote total and there was only about a three percent chance of McCain winning, according to the betting odds. It looked to be almost a certainty that Iowa was not going to be a swing state and Bob had the potential to do very well in Iowa if we would just have some ability to promote the campaign using traditional media and use public relations to promote our advertising campaign. After all, Bob was born in Iowa City. The local media would love to discuss that piece of information.

After I was given a green light on the Iowa advertising plan and spent a lot of my time pursuing rates and plans, I was told we could not fundraise through the Barr campaign for our own advertising. Talk about a clear violation of the 1:10:100 rule. Those of you who have worked with me know that I rarely get angry and am usually exceptionally calm. After I was told this, I was livid and strongly considered telling the national staff what they could do. Fortunately, our Iowa supporters and volunteers never found out about the decision of the national campaign staff.

Ballot Access:

The state organizations must be strengthened in order to decrease the time and effort required to gather signatures. In 2012, ballot access must improve. Ballot access is one area in which the party is doing worse compared to previous years. In 2004, the Libertarian Presidential nominee was on the ballot in 48 states plus Washington D.C. In 2008, we were only on the ballot in 45 states and not Washington D.C.

There definitely needed to be better coordination with the Libertarian Party on ballot access. There also needed to be quick decisive decisions made as to what states we were going to target and what states we were going to give up on. I remember that Mike Ferguson was going to drive up to Des Moines, Iowa where the Libertarian Party of Iowa was holding an Executive Committee meeting. At the last minute, he called and told me that he was going to have to go to West Virginia to petition and mentioned sending Vice-Presidential candidate Root in. Instead of flying in Wayne, I had Mike set up a conference call with Wayne, and Mike was kind enough to record a video. If we would have started West Virginia earlier we could have possibly got on the ballot. If we had stuck with the decision not to go to West Virginia we would have saved a lot of volunteer and financial resources. Another example was the Louisiana ballot access. Bob should have been on the ballot in Louisiana and I am informed that he likely would have been, with better coordination.

The attempt by the Barr campaign to kick John McCain and Barack Obama off the Texas ballot generated great publicity and allowed the American people to view the hypocrisy of ballot access laws. In fact, this was discussed on a radio station, not talk radio, I was listening to.

Communications:

The Barr campaign had a very good idea. They allowed the state coordinators to call in on a weekly conference call to discuss strategy. They also allowed us to use the conference call to call our county coordinators in our states. This allowed us to share ideas and communicate more effectively with each other.

Materials:

Another bad thing about announcing late is that the campaign does not have things like brochures ready. It wasn't until July that I got the brochures to hand out. It was also suggested that we would be charged by the campaign for obtaining the campaign materials to distribute; however, the campaign did send me materials to distribute at no cost to me personally. Unfortunately, volunteers were forced to buy their own yard signs. I hated to tell supporters that I would give them bumper stickers, but I had no yard signs for them.

I caught a lot of hell over the fact that "Libertarian" was not mentioned on many of the campaign materials. There was a legitimate reason for that. It is easier to convince someone to vote for you if they don't feel excluded by party names. The thing that concerned me was that there was no volunteer form to fill out and send in on the brochures.

Media:

In 2004, I saw Gary Nolan on Fox News and heard that Michael Badnarik won the nomination on the morning radio news break, and listened to Michael on Mancow. The Gary Nolan interview was my first introduction to the Libertarian Party. Compare this with 2008. In 2008, I heard Bob Barr being mentioned shortly before he announced his exploratory campaign, immediately after he announced, during the radio news breaks numerous times, then saw Bob in the news papers numerous times, and even on the front page of Yahoo a few times. In fact, my cousin even told me, "I saw your candidate Matt Barr on T.V. the other day." Well, at least he got the last name correct. I also received a call from a family member informing me that they watched Bob on Glenn Beck. In 2004, nobody I talked to had heard of Michael Badnarik. The massive increase in media attention was by far the biggest success of the Barr campaign and something we should strive for in future campaigns.

Reason Debates:

In 2004, Libertarian Party Presidential candidate Michael Badnarik was arrested while trying to debate President Bush and Senator Kerry. Congressman Barr did not go that far; however, he did debate Senator McCain and President Obama live on Reason.com's website. The technology needs to be improved upon. It would have been better if Bob could have paused live television to respond instead of just talking over them, and the video stream did go down temporarily, but this was a great strategy. I hope the 2012 campaign improves upon the technology and decides to allow for debate like Bob did if the candidate is not invited to the official debates.

The Barr campaign also did a superb job of taking advantage of the massive government bailouts of financial institutions.

Professionalism:

The Barr campaign almost perfected professional looking logos, videos, materials, and website design. This was a huge benefit to the campaign.

There were a couple of times when I had to shake my head. For example, the press release regarding the death of Senator Jesse Helms, which caused one major supporter (who helped convince me to give my delegate vote to Barr) to, at least temporarily, withdraw his volunteer support of the campaign and possibly his monetary support. Another time was when supporters were asked to call talk radio shows and promote the campaign. Someone posted the following comment on Last Free Voice in response:

"We're getting reports now from that big jet crash out at the airport. Dozens are feared dead. I have on the line a caller who is at the scene. Tell me, caller, what do you see?"

"It's terrible, Kent! Bodies and plane wreckage everywhere. That's a great issue to discuss, but let me tell you about a real choice in the race for the presidency, Bob Barr."

"Excuse me?"

"You know, Bob Barr, the Libertarian candidate for President. His website Bob Barr 2008 dot–"

"I'm being told by my producers that was a crank caller. Let's go to Mr. Baba Booey on line 2…"

Source: http://lastfreevoice.wordpress.com/2008/08/06/60-seconds-for-bob-how-to-defraud-call-screeners-and-piss-off-talk-radio-hosts/#comments

Qualifications to run:

No one person ever suggested to me that Bob was not qualified to run for President. In fact, some people even told me they believed he had more legislative experience than President Obama had.

Racism:

During the 2008 Ron Paul Presidential campaign, Ron Paul refused to return money donated by a member of the White Nationalist Community, Stormfront. This, along with the newsletters, in my opinion, did great harm to the Paul campaign. When an endorsement of Bob Barr was posted on a separatist website, Barr campaign manager Russ Verney released the following statement:

"The Barr campaign is not going to be a vehicle for every fringe and hate group to promote itself. We do not want and will not accept the support of haters. Anyone with love in their heart for our country and for every resident of our country regardless of race, religion, nationality or sexual orientation is welcome with open arms."

"Tell the haters I said don't let the door hit you on the backside on your way out! "

Source: http://www.reason.com/blog/show/126790.html

I believe the reply posted by Mr. Verney above kept the campaign on message.

Swing-State Strategy:

One strategy that it appears both the 2004 campaign of Michael Badnarik and the 2008 campaign of Bob Barr used was targeting swing states. In my opinion, it didn't work either time, and when you target swing states you might get more media attention; however, voters who think they can decide the outcome of the election don't end up voting for a third party candidate. In the future, I would like to see the Libertarian candidate target safe states in order to try and increase their vote totals that way.

Volunteer Support:

In my opinion, one of the biggest factors that harmed the Barr campaign was the fact that Bob announced so late that he did not have time to develop a campaign structure similar to ones I assisted with, like National Mobilization Facilitator and later on, as Chief of Staff for the Phillies campaign. With the Phillies campaign, we had coordinators in a little over twenty of the states, one in D.C., and I had plans to name the rest shortly after the convention ended. Running for President takes a lot of planning and when a candidate decides impulsively at the last minute that they don't have the time to put together a staff and fix any problems before the general election. This should be a lesson to the future Libertarian Party delegates about nominating candidates who have not had time to build their campaign organizations. In November, at the end of the campaign, it appears the Barr campaign was about where the Phillies campaign was at in May, in regards to the number of state coordinators.

As Iowa coordinator, you would likely think I would have had access to the Iowa volunteer lists. I did not. In order to contact the Iowa volunteers I had to write an e-mail and send it to my regional coordinator, and he had to send it to someone on the national staff to actually send out. Sometimes it would take almost a week of fighting to get an e-mail blast sent out. I really did like the e-mail blast idea. In fact, it made my job of getting talking points out very effective; however, I think in hindsight it should have been just a small part of the volunteer contact strategy.

Perhaps the biggest failure, in my opinion, was immediately following the campaign. The day after the election, I wrote an e-mail to be sent out to all the Iowa supporters thanking them and asking them to get involved with the Libertarian Party of Iowa. It never went out.

No state pages on website: One thing we learned in 2008 was the ability to use the Internet for more than just porn and eBay; it can be used to promote campaign events. I first started seeing this when I was working with the Phillies Presidential campaign. Our MySpace coordinator was posting events to the Phillies MySpace calendar. People started showing up to events because they saw it on our MySpace profile. That is why we started the process of state pages during the Phillies campaign. After the nomination we would be ready to promote news and events in every state.

During the Barr campaign, it would have been great to set up state pages to inform supporters about events that were happening and to distribute news like polling numbers, door-to-door efforts, and petition deadlines.

Wayne Root

It has been suggested to me that the second biggest failure, behind the swing-state strategy, in the Barr campaign is that they did not properly utilize the media skills and abilities of Vice-Presidential candidate Wayne Root by trying to get Wayne on more talk radio programs.

The article wouldn't be complete without mentioning some of my own personal mistakes in the campaign. I predicted we could get a coordinator in all five of Iowa's Congressional Districts. We only finished with three. I also believed I could get around two percent of the vote with the limited resources I had. While we received a higher percentage and more votes than any Libertarian Presidential candidate since Ed Clark in 1980, we did not come anywhere close to getting the two percent I believed we could receive. I also failed in my project to get Bob to Iowa.

For Immediate Release
Monday, September 13, 2010

PORTER CHALLENGES MAURO AND SCHULTZ TO PROMISE TO CUT PAY

Des Moines, IA- The Iowa Secretary of State currently makes $103,000 a year – nearly three times the average Iowan's income – which Libertarian candidate Jake Porter finds outrageous.

"I challenge Mauro and Schultz to promise to cut their pay by at least 10%. I have promised that if I am elected I will cut my pay by more than half from $103,000 to $50.000 a year," Porter said. "In July,

Mauro refused to even cut his pay by 10% and Schultz, the Republican candidate, is not even talking about the issue and is instead focusing on growing the government and other issues the Secretary of State has no Constitutional control over."

Porter faces Democrat Michael Mauro and Republican Matt Schultz in the November election. He's the nominee of the Libertarian Party, Iowa's third largest political party.

-30-
about 130 words

Contact Information:
Tim Tinkle, Chief of Staff
media@jakeporter.org
Phone Number

For Immediate Release
Monday, July 22, 2013

PORTER ANNOUNCES RUN FOR SECRETARY OF STATE

Council Bluffs, Iowa-Jake Porter has declared his intention to run for Iowa Secretary of State in the 2014 election as a Libertarian.

Porter, 25, was the 2010 Libertarian nominee for Secretary of State. In 2010, Porter received 33,854 votes in the general election, covering the margin of Republican Matt Schultz's victory over Democrat Michael Mauro.

Porter earned his Bachelors Degree in Business Administration from AIB College of Business in Des Moines. After college, Porter moved to Nebraska where he worked as a retail store manager. Today, Porter lives in Council Bluffs and handles customer care issues for a large Internet corporation in Omaha. In addition to his private sector work, Porter has managed and advised several political campaigns. Porter believes his hard work and experience make him a perfect fit for the job. "The Secretary of State primarily deals with business and elections which are two areas I know first-hand. Additionally, my management experience allows me to effectively and efficiently manage the Secretary of State's office."

Although Porter has own political positions, he has questioned his opponents for their heavy ties to partisan politics. "As Secretary of State, I would not endorse any political candidate like Matt Schultz did when he supported Rick Santorum for President. Additionally, I do not have ties to one of the two major political parties like Brad Anderson does. Unlike Anderson, I have never advised or worked for John Edwards or President Obama. We need someone who is independent of the two major political parties to act as a referee and that is the type of candidate I am." Porter said.

In addition to keeping the office independent and transparent, Porter wants to make starting a business in Iowa easier. His highest priority is maintaining safe and secure elections without disenfranchising the voters of Iowa.

Porter will file paperwork with the Iowa Ethics and Disclosure Board later in the week. He has already assembled a campaign organization. The campaign plans to run an active campaign primarily using radio, television, newspaper, and Internet advertising to gain name recognition among Iowa voters.

For more information about Jake Porter please visit:
www.jakeporter.org

–30–

about 340 words.

Contact Information:

Tim Tinkle, Chief of Staff

media@jakeporter.org

Phone Number

www.ingramcontent.com/pod-product-compliance
Lightning Source LLC
Chambersburg PA
CBHW070907290526
45795CB00001B/233